ideals
MOTHER'S DAY

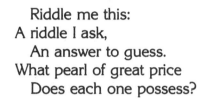

Riddle me this:
A riddle I ask,
    An answer to guess.
What pearl of great price
    Does each one possess?

A token I give
    To help with this game,
Love beyond measure—
    It's all in a name.

Riddle me right,
    There can be no other.
God's greatest gift?
    The answer is Mother.

Sara Bren

Editorial Director, James Kuse

Managing Editor, Ralph Luedtke

Editor/Ideals, Colleen Callahan Gonring

Associate Editor, Linda Robinson

Production Editor/Manager, Richard Lawson

Photographic Editor, Gerald Koser

Copy Editor, Norma Barnes

Art Editor, Duane Weaver

ISBN 0-89542-331-6 295

IDEALS—Vol. 37, No. 3 April MCMLXXX. IDEALS (ISSN 0019-137X) is published eight times a year,
January, February, April, June, July, September, October, November
by IDEALS PUBLISHING CORPORATION, 11315 Watertown Plank Road, Milwaukee, Wis. 53226
Second class postage paid at Milwaukee, Wisconsin. Copyright © MCMLXXX by IDEALS PUBLISHING CORPORATION.
Postmaster, please send form 3579 to Ideals Publishing Corporation, 175 Community Drive, Great Neck, New York, 11025
All rights reserved. Title IDEALS registered U.S. Patent Office.
Published Simultaneously in Canada.

ONE YEAR SUBSCRIPTION—eight consecutive issues as published—only $15.95
TWO YEAR SUBSCRIPTION—sixteen consecutive issues as published—only $27.95
SINGLE ISSUES—only $2.95

The Hand That Rocks the Cradle

Blessings on the hand of woman!
    Angels guard its strength and grace,
In the palace, cottage, hovel,
    Oh, no matter where the place.
Would that never storms assailed it,
    Rainbows ever gently curled,
For the hand that rocks the cradle
    Is the hand that rules the world.

Infancy's the tender fountain,
    Power may with beauty flow;
Mother's first to guide the streamlets,
    From them souls unresting grow . . .
Grow on for the good or evil,
    Sunshine streamed or evil-hurled,
For the hand that rocks the cradle
    Is the hand that rules the world.

Woman, how divine your mission
    Here upon our natal sod!
Keep, oh, keep the young heart open
    Always to the breath of God!
All true trophies of the ages
    Are from mother-love impearled,
For the hand that rocks the cradle
    Is the hand that rules the world.

Blessings on the hand of woman!
    Fathers, sons, and daughters cry,
And the sacred song is mingled
    With the worship in the sky . . .
Mingles where no tempest darkens,
    Rainbows evermore are hurled,
For the hand that rocks the cradle
    Is the hand that rules the world.

William Ross Wallace

Lullabies

Dorothy Berliner Commins

Lullabies are love songs. Sometimes they are gay and sometimes they are sad; but, whatever the mood, they are always tender. They are the expression of one of the deepest emotions of the human spirit. A lullaby is born in a mother's heart to live on in the child's memory, for a lifetime and even longer, for lullabies are passed on from generation to generation.

The world today is changing swiftly. No pattern of family life in any part of the world can be definitive. Lives do not set like concrete, nor is folklore cast in bronze. The characteristic of folk music has been its flexibility, its power to keep an identity while borrowing and assimilating elements from other cultures. Today diverse and distant cultures touch upon each other, for technological development has made time, distance, and natural barriers dwindle.

One day we may find ourselves members of one world. This will be only the fulfillment of the human condition for, in a real sense, there has been one world since the beginning of human history, the family of man. Mother love is universal. It survives in folk lullabies all over the world. Though cultures may change, nations rise and fall, languages evolve or vanish, there will always be lullabies. [Mothers' lullabies] preserve something of the past and at the same time look forward to the future.

To the child in the cradle or the mother's arms, these love songs are the first melodies heard. They are sung at an hour when the mother's presence and the sound of her voice mean safety and peace and comfort. While the mother rocks her child back and forth, old melodies are recalled and return. She sings what she remembers hearing as a baby, what her mother sang to her, and her mother's mother. New words are added. Slight changes in the melody occur, but the substance and the spirit are unchanging.

The character of most lullabies can be identified with the history of a people. They belong to no composer. They belong to all mothers of a nation or a culture. Like all folklore, the lullaby came into being spontaneously. Need for it gave it birth, and it flowered with a vitality all its own. It has always been so with folklore, whether the form of expression is a nursery rhyme, a fairy tale, an epic or a legend. The first tellers of tales and singers of songs will be forever unknown. Much must have been lost and much must have been gained as the new, added to the old, kept alive the folk song and story. The familiar analogy to the tree in the forest is apt. From year to year its fruit is plucked or falls; its leaves are shed, and often branches wither away or are struck down. But the sturdy tree has deep roots in the soil, representing the past. New seasons continually bring new branches, new leaves, blossoms, and fruit.

Of all folklore, the lullaby may have the simplest and most direct appeal. It needs no words, and even when words are used, the infant is usually too young to understand them. The sounds and rhythms suffice. Whatever the words mean, it is the mother alone who really appreciates them. The thought of a cradle swaying perilously on a treetop would only terrify an infant. Wind blowing and the whole bough breaking and falling with a crash would probably be good raw material for nightmares if the child really grasped the meaning of the words. What can a Greek baby, for example, know or care about ruling over Alexandria, Cairo, or Constantinople, though the mother blithely promises these to him if he will only go to sleep? Gentle rhythms convey all the meaning he needs at the moment—and all the conquest. However, the words have a very real meaning to the mother. They express the hopes mothers always cherish for their children.

It can be assumed that most lullabies originated among the peasantry and the working classes. Mothers of the aristocracy were seldom required to devote themselves exclusively to their infants. They could easily engage wet nurses and governesses. These servants came from the land and brought with them the traditions and beliefs and songs of the people. They lulled infants to sleep in their arms while they swayed in gentle, rhythmic movement. And when hands could not be spared from the many chores that fall to the lot of women, the foot-rocking cradle was invented.

Even when cradles are not used (as, for example, in Japan and in some parts of Asia and Africa) the infant is usually strapped to the mother's back so that her hands will be free for work in the fields or at home. No one can complain that a song interferes with work in progress. The mind can wander free and the voice can rise and fall in tender cadences while the hands are busy.

How can one account for the persistent note of great sadness running through the words and melodies of many lullabies? Prospects less than promising exist for many a child in his crib. Since time began mothers have seen their bright dreams for their children shattered. Sons have marched off to wars; others have lived lives of grinding proverty, of hopeless illness and defeat. But equally important are the visions of a better life and happier times which enter into lullabies. Cares are banished and poverty is forgotten. Courage and gaiety replace longing and despair. Even the song shifts in mood. Lightness and charm come into the melody. The lullaby is worthy of a place with all the other treasures of man's endeavor which have been passed on to posterity.

Rock-a-by Baby, on the Treetop

Rock-a-by baby, on the treetop,
When the wind blows, the cradle will rock,
When the bough breaks, the cradle will fall,
And down will come baby, cradle and all.

Although the words of "Rock-a-by-Baby" had long been familiar as a Mother Goose rhyme, the credit for setting these words to music is generally given to Mrs. Effic Canning Carlton, who is said to have composed it on the porch of her father's summer home in 1874. It received widespread popularity when it was used as one of the songs in Denman Thompson's production of *The Old Homestead*. A good deal of controversy, however, attends Mrs. Carlton's claim. Evidence indicates that the melody existed long before Mrs. Carlton joined it to the words to make the lullaby which is now so well known. One story she tells is particularly interesting. She reports that in 1854 her parents found an Indian squaw who had been injured and they took her into their house and nursed her. When the squaw recovered, she took a fancy to the baby of the family and often sang the melody of what we now call "Rock-a-by-Baby." Melodies travel wide and far, invisibly and more swiftly than words. Perhaps the Indian woman had heard it from some white settler, and it is quite possible that Mrs. Carlton as a child heard this melody in Boston and later lifted it from some vague, unconscious memory. In any case, she honestly believed that it was her own creation and she certainly deserves credit for bringing together melody and words to make one of the most popular of all lullabies.

'Tis Good to Love

'Tis, oh, so very good to love
A child within our care,
To satisfy a little soul
So very sweet and fair,
To hold him tightly in our arms
And touch his tiny hand,
Then lend assurance to his heart
That he might understand.

'Tis good to love a little one
All soft and warm and dear,
To talk to him so quietly
That he shall know no fear,
A precious little bit of life
That God has bid you keep,
To love him, oh, so tenderly
In waking hours or sleep.

There is no dearer joy on earth
Than just a baby's smile,
'Tis this alone can fill your day
With everything worthwhile;
And you shall know this treasured gift
God sent you from above,
And as you teach this little one
You'll find 'tis good to love.

Garnett Ann Schultz

What Is It Worth?

What is it worth, that tiny hand
You often hold so tight,
That small, little face with its bright, little smile
That seems to make everything right,
One little heart and two rosy cheeks,
The chatter that lasts through the day,
The hours of quiet when nighttime arrives,
The moments of laughter and play?

What is it worth, that small, golden head
And that dear, little turned up nose,
Soft, little fingers that never are still,
A fragrance as sweet as a rose,
One precious kiss that enters your heart
And means all the world you shall find,
Small dancing feet that never once stop,
An active and bright little mind?

Worries and heartaches, troubles and woes,
Yet laughter to last through it all,
It takes but a hug from two tiny arms
And quickly you're seven feet tall,
One little angel all smiling and gay,
No richer treasure on earth,
Yours from God's heaven, to have and to love,
Never knowing just what it is worth.

Garnett Ann Schultz

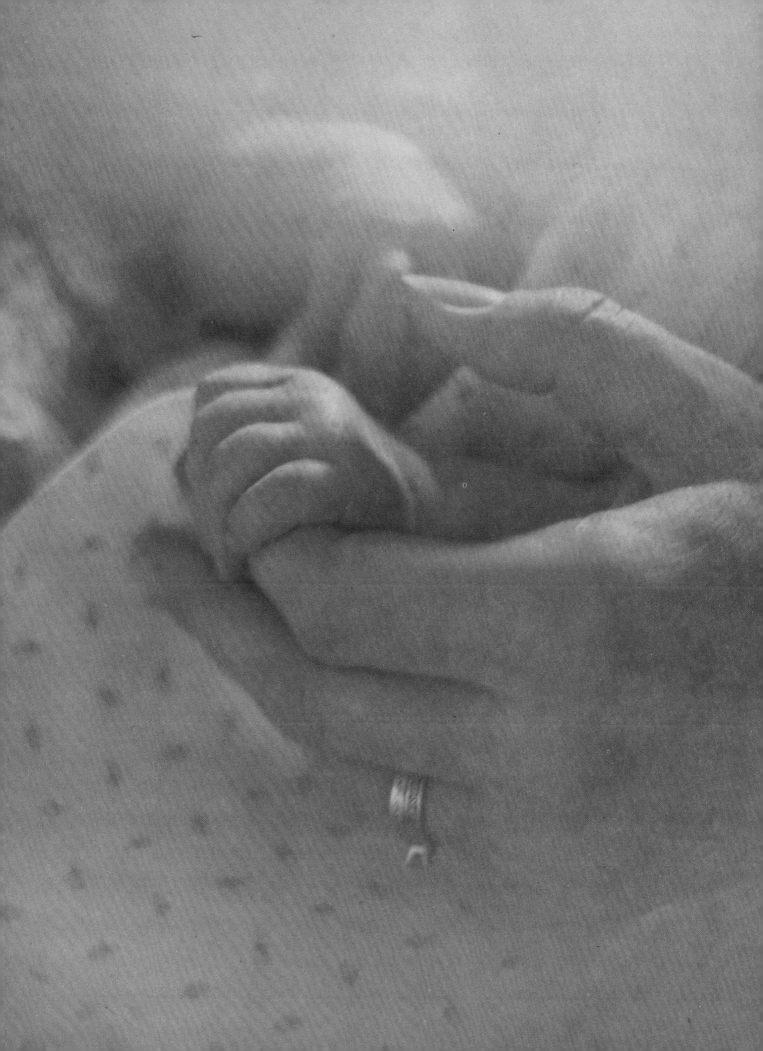

Helen Steiner Rice

"Your writings are the most inspiring I have ever read. . . . They have consoled me as nothing else has." "The verse is so simple . . . anyone can understand it; it inspires . . . and gives . . . meaning." Expressions such as these come often in letters of thanks to Helen Steiner Rice, one of America's foremost writers of inspirational verse. A native of Lorain, Ohio, Mrs. Rice began her working career as an Associate of the Ohio Public Service Company. Her talents soon raised her to the ranks of the highest paid women executives in the electric power industry. In a short time, she was able to open her own lecturing service, touring the nation and attempting to develop a better understanding of the role of women in business. It was while speaking at a bankers' convention that she met her husband, who, unfortunately, died unexpectedly a few years later. Those who knew her talents asked her to join the greeting card business, where she worked diligently for the meaningful expression of sentiment. In the fall of 1960, Lawrence Welk, well-known orchestra leader, chose to read one of Mrs. Rice's poems, "The Priceless Gift of Christmas," on his nationwide television program. Hundreds wrote asking for more, and since then her audience has grown and spread around the world. The Library of Congress selected her first hardcover book for translation into braille. Many of her works have been printed in foreign languages. In a world in need of comfort, Mrs. Rice's poems continue to touch people, giving them solace and hope with simple expressions of faith and the love of God.

For One Who Gives So Much To Others

It's not the things that can be bought
That are life's richest treasure;
It's just the little "heart gifts"
That money cannot measure.
A cheerful smile, a friendly word,
A sympathetic nod
Are priceless little treasures
From the storehouse of our God.
They are the things that can't be bought
With silver or with gold,
For thoughtfulness and kindness
And love are never sold.

They are the priceless things in life
For which no one can pay,
And the giver finds rich recompense
In giving them away.
And who on earth gives more away
And does more good for others
Than understanding, kind and wise
And selfless, loving mothers,
Who ask no more than just the joy
Of helping those they love
To find in life the happiness
That they are dreaming of.

Where There Is Love

Where there is love the heart is light,
Where there is love the day is bright,
Where there is love there is a song
To help when things are going wrong.
Where there is love there is a smile
To make all things seem more worthwhile;
Where there is love there's quiet peace,
A tranquil place where turmoils cease.
Love changes darkness into light
And makes the heart take "wingless flight."
And mothers have a special way
Of filling homes with love each day,
And when the home is filled with love
You'll always find God spoken of,
And when a family "prays together,"
That family also "stays together."
And once again a mother's touch
Can mold and shape and do so much
To make this world a better place
For every color, creed and race,
For when man walks with God again,
There shall be peace on earth for men.

Mother is a Word Called Love

Mother is a word called Love.
And all the world is mindful of
The love that's given and shown to others
Is different from the love of mothers,
For mothers play the leading roles
In giving birth to little souls,
For though "small souls" are heaven-sent,
And we realize they're only lent,
It takes a mother's loving hands
And her gentle heart that understands
To mold and shape this little life
And shelter it through storm and strife.
No other love than mother love
Could do the things required of
The one to whom God gives the keeping
Of His wee lambs, awake or sleeping—
So mothers are a "special race"
God sent to earth to take His place,
And Mother is a lovely name
That even saints are proud to claim.

The Love of a Mother

It takes a mother's love
To make a house a home,
A place to be remembered,
No matter where we roam.
It takes a mother's patience
To bring a child up right,
And her courage and her cheerfulness
To make a dark day bright.
It takes a mother's thoughtfulness
To mend the heart's deep "hurts,"
And her skill and her endurance
To mend little socks and shirts.

It takes a mother's kindness
To forgive us when we err,
To sympathize in trouble
And bow her head in prayer.
It takes a mother's wisdom
To recognize our needs
And to give us reassurance
By her loving words and deeds.
It takes a mother's endless faith,
Her confidence and trust
To guide us through the pitfalls
Of selfishness and lust.
And that is why in all this world
There could not be another
Who could fulfill God's purpose
As completely as
A mother!

For Mother
On Mother's Day

"No other love
Than mother love
Could do the things
Required of
The one to whom
God gives the keeping
Of His wee lambs,
Awake or sleeping."

Mom's Special Day

It's Mom's day! Why not help her start it in a special way? The entire family can join in the fun of preparing breakfast for mother—while she catches a few more winks or relaxes over coffee. She may request her favorites, but, if surprise is part of the plan, try cooking up something new, such as . . .

BAKED SCRAMBLED EGGS

  6 eggs, beaten
 1/3 c. milk
  1 t. salt
 1/8 t. pepper
 1/4 lb. American cheese, cubed

Mix ingredients in order given. Bake in a well-buttered casserole in a 350° oven for 30 minutes, or until puffy and when a knife is inserted, it comes out clean.

BAKED CANADIAN BACON

  3 lbs. Canadian bacon
  1 orange, cut into thin slices
 1/2 c. molasses
 1/4 c. water
 1/2 c. orange juice
 1/4 c. sugar
 1/4 t. dry mustard
     Whole cloves

Remove casing from bacon and place, fat side up, in an open pan. Bake in a 325° oven for 2 hours. Remove from the oven and attach orange slices to bacon with cloves. Mix remaining ingredients. Pour over bacon and bake, basting often, at 325° for 30 minutes.

COFFEE CAKE SUPREME

 1/2 lb. butter or margarine
  1 c. sugar
  3 eggs
  3 c. sifted flour
 2½ t. baking powder
 1/2 t. salt
  8 ozs. sour cream (or cream substitute)
 1/2 t. baking soda
  1 t. vanilla

Cream butter and sugar. Add eggs and beat until light and fluffy. Sift flour, baking powder and salt several times. Combine baking soda and sour cream. Add alternately with flour, ending with flour. Add vanilla. Layer in bundt pan with streusel and bake.

STREUSEL

 3/4 c. brown sugar
 1/2 t. cinnamon
 3/4 c. chopped nuts

Grease a bundt pan well and dust with flour. Mix streusel ingredients together and sprinkle pan with a third of the mixture, then a third of cake batter, repeating layers in thirds. Bake in 350° oven 1 hour. Invert pan onto cookie or cake rack to cool.

Mom's Breakfast Treat

It has become traditional in our household for the children to make "breakfast in bed" for Mother on Mother's Day. They figure it's no more than right, since she makes breakfast, lunch and dinner for them 364 *other* days of the year.

Like many traditions—firecrackers on July 4th, pumpkins on Halloween, and sumptuous feasts on Thanksgiving Day—Mother's Day traditions may have minor drawbacks.

For some reason, whenever they decide to make a meal, our eleven children insist on serving gargantuan portions. They make enough food to feed a brigade of truck drivers. My wife is not offered a *choice* of bacon and eggs, pancakes, muffins, waffles, French toast and coffee—she is served *lots* of *each*!

One particular Mother's Day that stands out is the time red-headed daughter Bridget decided to personally prepare blueberry muffins for her mother's special day. Bridget was always the clean one. The night before Mother's Day the "Red Fox," as I had dubbed her, energetically cleaned the oven with Brillo pads. Scrub, scrub, rub, rub—Bridget made sure that oven would be shiny-bright to accept her Mother's Day muffins.

The next morning the kids came trouping up the stairs, each carrying something for Mom's breakfast. One brought orange juice in a giant goblet that normally served as a vase; another carted a half-loaf of toast. Another balanced a stack of nine pancakes, another brought a plate of eggs. A fifth offspring displayed a plate holding a half-pound of bacon; another clutched a pot of coffee. And finally, Bridget fiercely, but proudly, gripped her pan of one dozen muffins.

The king-sized bed was hardly big enough to hold breakfast!

Grudgingly, the kids agreed that I could partake—but I was to be sure to let Mother eat all she wanted *first*!

What with the butter, the syrup and the eggs . . . everything went swimmingly. Then . . . we reached for one of Bridget's beautiful brown muffins, buttered and bit into one. The "Red Fox" proudly stood by, watching intently!

I don't know what a Brillo pad tastes like, 'cause I never ate one. But what I had just bitten into tasted like what I *figured* a Brillo pad would. Mary quickly reached for the coffee, maintaining a loyal smile. I hopped out of bed and ran for the bathroom. Grabbing a glass of water, I washed out the remnants of the soapy-tasting muffin. Mary gamely ate the whole thing!

As I emerged and rejoined the group, I suggested the kids permit their dear mother to eat her fine meal in peace. When they left, I hid the muffins in a wastebasket, dressed and sneaked the container out to the garbage. By this time, Mary had risen—looking the color of a muffin—and gone down to the kitchen. She opened the oven and looked inside.

What had happened was—Bridget had indeed cleaned, scrubbed and Brillo-padded the oven. There remained a layer of soap along the grates and on the side-walls. What Bridget *didn't* do was *rinse it out*!

From what I hear, baked goods have a tendency to absorb odors and aromas from an oven while being baked, and for that reason ovens must be *rinsed* each time they're cleaned.

Mary never let on, all these years!

Now, at 24, Bridget is old enough to handle the news. She might even be able to discreetly tip off her own offspring to the hazards of baking muffins in an oven scoured with Brillo pads. And with love!

Gale Brennan

To Love a Child

She is not yet nine years old, this daughter of mine, and already she has begun to grow away from me. I watch her practicing a headstand for a gymnastics show. Seeing me watching her, she asks, "Do I look all right?"

"Perfect," I assure her.

"You always say that," she replies calmly. If she were upright, I know she'd shrug.

Jennifer seems to be more confident lately, *cool* almost, as if emotionally she no longer needs me as much. And as she withdraws, I suddenly feel unaccountably angry at this child who is becoming whole enough to grow away from me.

Once there was a closeness, a warm physical and emotional bond with my only daughter. When she was four and five she'd go to her room to play, but every short while she'd return for a drink of water or a cut to be fixed—really to reassure me as much as herself. "I am here." she seemed to say. "I knew you'd want to see me." It used to be that her bedroom door, closed so often to her brothers, was always open to me. Lately, she expects that I will knock. And when I do, she no longer gleefully pulls me inside, closing the door and enticing me into a game. Now, she waits at the door, seeming to ask silently what it is I wish.

I ask her what she plans to do in the gymnastics show. "Floor routines and the ropes," Jennifer replies. "I decided against the balance beam because the girls who do that are show-offs. Look . . . " She does a backward walkover for me, her legs coming down expertly, her arms flipped out in exaggeration of the gymnast's pose, her face reflecting calculated indifference. "That's what they look like," she says. Suddenly her serious concentration is broken; she gives me an unexpected smile and rushes off to wrestle with the dog.

I wonder how she has acquired this independence, self-confidence and security at such a young age. Certainly I have worked to help her attain it. Certainly I wish it for her. But a part of me mourns for the simple, utter dependency of her babyhood. Must it always be so? Does every mother work hard to provide a way for her child—and then resent it when the child attains what *she* desired? I know a part of me withdraws from her when I sense her competency, her seeming lack of need.

When Jennifer was very small, she was reckless with things others were cautious about. She climbed the spruce tree that rose above the roof of our house. She punched back when her brothers got rough with her. She learned to swim in an icy lake when she was only four, boarded a plane alone, to visit her grandmother, when she was five. And today, as she verges on nine years old, the outer competence is reflected in inner things. Her teachers comment on her sensitivity, the calm she holds within.

She brings home stacks of books from the library, studying, she tells me, to be a veterinarian. On other days she thinks she will be a teacher, a doctor, a gymnast. She is tender with small living things, roughshod with things she says don't count. Early this week she was busy building a nest on the ground. She carefully rounded, molded and patted it into shape. When finished, it was big enough for an eagle, at least. "Just something for the birds," Jennifer told me gravely.

About her room, and even her person, there is no such care. She dismisses my urgings that she dress neatly for classes. "School is not a beauty contest," she tells me coolly.

I suppose, if the truth were known, I would have Jennifer be the living, breathing, walking resolution of every conflict I have ever had. When I was eight, I was trying to clean a run-down house for a mother who was too tired to do it when she came home from work; trying to keep order in a room I shared with two sisters and a grandmother. But Jennifer cares little about order or her beautiful room.

When I was eight, I had a painful operation and was told I was too old to cry anymore. Jennifer cries from hurt, physical or emotional, sometimes for an hour or more. "I like to cry," she says, so much more aware of what goes on inside her than I have ever been.

It seems strange that I am proud of the self-knowledge and independence of this child when, at the same time, another part of me shouts silently, "You have gone too far!" Is this a universal conflict of parenthood? For I find I am proud that she does not need me, but resent her when she does not want me. I teach her self-confidence, then envy her serenity. I nurture her strength, then am angry when she uses it to fight against me. And always a part of me is fiercely joyful for this child who is strong enough to separate herself from me. For in spite of the pain, I would not have it differently.

Patricia Hermes

GIVE AN IDEALS
GIFT SUBSCRIPTION
THIS FATHER'S DAY

SAVE 33% OFF THE SINGLE ISSUE PRICE

So don't delay! Mail the postage-paid coupon below today!

( ) Please send a 1 year subscription to IDEALS (8 issues for $15.95) a savings of $7.65 off the single issue price—to my special friend or relative listed below.

( ) Please send a 2 year subscription to IDEALS (16 issues for $27.95) a savings of $19.25 off the single issue price—to my special friend or relative listed below.

Outside Continental U.S. - Add $2.00 Per Subscription Year For Postage & Handling

Gift Name _____

Address _____

City _____ State _____ Zip _____

Your Name _____

Address _____

City _____ State _____ Zip _____

( ) Bill me.   ( ) I enclose check/money order.

Please charge: ( ) Master Charge   ( ) BA/Visa

Exp. Date _____ Bank _____

Card # _____

Signature _____

C003

SUBSCRIBE TO IDEALS TODAY!

Full color photos Poetry & prose

SAVE 33% OFF Single Issue Cost!

So don't delay! Mail the postage-paid coupon below today!

☐ Please enter my 1-year subscription (8 issues) for only $15.95—a savings of $7.65 off the single issue price.

☐ Please enter my 2-year subscription (16 issues) for only $27.95—a saving of $19.25 off the single issue price.

Outside Continental U.S. - Add $2.00 Per Subscription Year For Postage & Handling

( ) Bill me.   ( ) I enclose check/money order.

Please charge: ( ) Master Charge   ( ) BA/Visa

Exp. Date _____ Bank _____

Card # _____

Signature _____

NAME _____

ADDRESS _____

CITY _____ STATE _____ ZIP _____

C003

BUSINESS REPLY CARD

FIRST CLASS   PERMIT NO. 5761   MILWAUKEE, WI

ideals

PUBLISHING CORPORATION

11315 WATERTOWN PLANK RD.

MILWAUKEE, WISCONSIN 53226

NO POSTAGE
NECESSARY
IF MAILED
IN THE
UNITED STATES

BUSINESS REPLY CARD

FIRST CLASS   PERMIT NO. 5761   MILWAUKEE, WI

ideals

PUBLISHING CORPORATION

11315 WATERTOWN PLANK RD.

MILWAUKEE, WISCONSIN 53226

IDEALS MAGAZINE—selected best of category among magazines by the Printing Industries of America in 1979/80.

By selecting Ideals for this prestigious award, the PIA has recognized a standard of publishing excellence that you, the Ideals subscriber, have known and enjoyed for over 35 years. Our subscribers merit the credit for this award because their demand for excellence and their continued loyalty aid in our determination to consistently improve the quality and appearance of IDEALS. During 1980 we will continue this tradition of excellence in order to maintain the quality you have come to expect. We thank you and invite you to share our success in the coming year.

nter the World of IDEALS!

Unique in a world of magazines featuring current events, motor trends and Hollywood glitter, *Ideals* offers both spiritual solace and sustenance for the mind. Beautiful color photography, delightful artwork, memorable prose and poetry are hallmarks of each issue. *Ideals* magazine is a treasured companion offering comfort, enjoyment and humor. Each of the eight issues published annually reflects the traditional values families have enjoyed throughout the years. Become a subscriber or give a gift subscription TODAY! (Each gift includes an attractive donor card!) *Ideals* . . . a magazine you will be proud to share with family and friends!

Perfect Moment

Somewhere along the road between "beginning" and "ending" there is a perfect moment for every living soul. There may possibly be more than one. But for the most part we are too busy, too young, too adult, too sophisticated, too this or too that to recognize it—and so the moment may be lost.

My perfect moment came when I was eight years old. I awoke one spring night to find moonlight flooding my room through the open window. It was so bright that I sat up in bed. There was no sound at all anywhere. The air was soft and heavy with the fragrance of pear blossoms and honeysuckle.

I crept out of bed and tiptoed softly out of the house. Eight-year-olds were not supposed to be astir at this hour. But I wanted to sit in the swing for a while and watch the moonlight. As I closed the door behind me, I saw my mother sitting on the porch steps. She looked up and smiled and, putting her finger to her lips, reached out with her other hand and drew me down beside her. I sat as close as I could and she put her arm around me.

The whole countryside was hushed and sleeping; no lights burned in any house. The moonlight was liquid silver and so bright we could see the dark outline of the woods a mile away. "Isn't it beautiful?" I whispered, and Mother's arm tightened about me.

Our shepherd dog, Frollo, came across the lawn and stretched himself out contentedly, his head on Mother's lap. For a long time we were all three perfectly still. The stars were pale and far away. Now and then the moonlight would strike a leaf of the Marechal Niel rose beside the porch and be caught for an instant in a dewdrop like a tiny living spark. The shrubs were hung with necklaces of diamonds, and the grass was sweet with dampness.

We knew that in the dark woods there were movement and sound among the wild things—the rabbits and squirrels, the oppossums and chipmunks, as they moved about in their own world.

And in the shadowy garden, and in the fields, things were growing. In the meadow the foal slept beside its mother, and nearby a young calf nuzzled its mother.

Very soon the blossoms on the fruit trees would lose their petals in a pink-and-white snowfall, and in their place the young fruit would appear. The wild-plum thicket would be filled with plums, round and glowing like tiny lanterns, made sweet by the sun and cool by the rain. In another field the young corn plants were inching their way upward. Melons would soon dot the trailing vines where now the squash-like blooms were replenishing their nectar in preparation for the onrush of bees in the morning.

In all this great brooding silence that seemed so infinite, the miracle of life was going on unseen and unheard. The bird sitting on her eggs in the mulberry tree carried out a divine purpose. The hills, undisturbed by passing centuries, proclaimed strength and grandeur. The moving of the stars, the planets, the countless worlds, all were governed and held within the safety of the omnipotent yet gentle hand of the Creator.

Mother pointed toward the cedar tree. "Look," she whispered softly, "that star seems caught in the branches."

As we watched it, suddenly from the topmost point of a pear tree a mockingbird burst into song. It was as though the joy that overflowed his heart must find expression. The notes were pure gold, free and clear and liquid as the moonlight, rising, falling, meltingly sweet. At times they were so soft as to be barely audible; then he would sing out, a rapturous profundo. As suddenly as it had begun, the concert ended and the night was silvery still again.

An eight-year-old does not analyze his thoughts; he may not even be aware that he is surrounded by infinity. But he sees a star impaled on the branch of a cedar tree, and knows pure ecstasy. He hears a mockingbird sing in the moonlight, and is filled with speechless joy. He feels his mother's arms about him, and knows complete security.

Gladys Bell

Confessions of an Officer in the Girl Scout Cookie Corps

No one was more surprised than I at being named Girl Scout Cookie Captain.

I had been in the restroom at the time of the promotion.

The moment following the announcement was rather exhilarating. Mothers crowding around me patting me on the back and whispering in my ear, "If you need anything, I'm in the book," and assuring me, "This is going to be the best year ever."

Then they were gone.

And there were twenty-five little girls looking at me to lead them into door-to-door combat.

"At ease," I said, "you may chew gum if you like."

One girl blew a bubble the size of a pink gall bladder. Another one looked at her watch and shifted her weight to the other foot. The others just stared.

"Now then," I said, "I think this is going to be a great experience for all of us. I'll help you and you can help me. I have only one question before you leave today. What's a Girl Scout Cookie Captain?"

"She sells cookies," said the girl with the gum.

"And where does she get the cookies?" I asked.

She shrugged, "From her own living room."

I nodded. "I see, and how do they get to her living room?"

"A big truck dumps them there," said another scout.

"Okay, girls, I'll get it all together and be in touch."

At home, I grabbed the phone book and began calling all of those wonderful people who had volunteered to help.

Frankly, I didn't realize there were so many of life's losers in one neighborhood.

"I'd love to help, but I'm allergic to children."

"We're only a one-phone family."

"Give me a break! I'm on a diet and I'm in remission."

"I'm volunteering so much now my husband reported me missing."

"Do I know you? Oh, *that* sister!"

The first meeting of the Girl Scout cookie army went well. We discussed on what day we would take orders and on what day they must report their sales to me. I, in turn, would process the order for the entire troop, and then there was nothing left to do but sit around and wait for C-Day to arrive.

It was about five weeks later when my husband nudged me out of a sound sleep one morning and said, "Do you hear something?"

"Ummm. What's it sound like?"

"Like a truck in our driveway."

We staggered to the window. By the headlights I saw them: full-grown men unloading carton after carton of cookies. "Where do you want them, lady?" they shouted.

I pointed to the living room.

When I told the girls the cookies were in they did a fantastic job of holding their emotions in restraint.

One cried, "There goes the skating party."

Another one slammed down her purse and said, "I wish I were dead."

And another one declared, "If it rains, I'm not delivering."

"It's all right, girls," I smiled, "don't hold back. You can show your excitement if you want to. Frankly, I'm just as choked up as you are. As I was telling my husband this morning as we breakfasted over 250 cartons of vanilla creams, 'This will show me to go to the restroom before I leave home.' "

The delivery of the cookies was a lot slower than I had anticipated. Hardly a day went by that I wasn't on the phone trying to contact one of the girls to pick up her cookies and deliver them.

"Hello, Marcia? I have the eighty-six boxes of cookies you ordered and . . . "

"My grandmother died."

"I'm sorry about that Marcia, but there are still the cookies."

"She was down for twenty-eight boxes."

"I see. Do you happen to know where I can get in touch with Debbie?"

"She moved."

"Where?"

"I promised I wouldn't tell you."

"What about Joanne?"

"She's dropped scouting. She's selling peanut brittle for the band now."

"Marcia! You tell the girls I'm up to my Girl Scout motto in cookies and I want them out of my living room by this weekend, do you hear?"

"Have you tried freezing them?" she asked mechanically.

"Freezing them! Sara Lee should have such a freezer!"

Stripping a captain of his rank in the cookie corps is not a pretty sight. I ripped off my armband, turned in the sign from my window that read "COOKIE HEADQUARTERS" and laid my golden badge on top of my yellow scarf.

"Do you have your records book?" asked the leader.

"I do," I said smartly. "It's all there. There are 143 cartons of cookies unaccounted for and $234 or $12.08 outstanding. It's hard to tell."

"Do you have anything to say?"

"Yes," I said, my voice faltering. "I want the record to show that I tried. When twenty-five girls literally vanished from the earth, I tried to dispose of the cookies myself. I sprinkled cookie crumbs on my salads, rolled them into pie crusts, coated pork chops in them, and packed them in lunches. I made paste out of them and mended books, rubbed them on my callouses and rough elbows, and wedged them under the door to keep it open.

"I sent them out with my bills each month, wore two of them as earrings, gave them as wedding gifts, and set glasses on them and pretended they were coasters.

"I put them under my pillow for good luck, made an abstract for the living room, dumped a canful over my compost and crumbled some of them up for kitty litter. I have a cookie rash on 97 percent of my body."

"Is that all?" asked the leader somberly.

"Yes, I'm finished."

As I started to leave the room, I could hear nominations being presented for next year's cookie captain.

I turned suddenly and took a front row seat. I couldn't take the chance of leaving the room again.

Erma Bombeck

Dedication of a day to mothers is relatively new to the United States. It was not until 1908 that the first such special day was held, but the tradition of setting aside a time for the public expression of love for mothers dates back to the ancient Greek empire. It was continued in pagan Rome and later by the early Christians in honor of the Virgin Mary. In England an ecclesiastical decree expanded the holiday to include all mothers. Perhaps because many of the early settlers in the United States were not members of the established church of England, they did not bring this celebration with them. It was not until the early 1900s that Miss Anna Jarvis succeeded, through a national letter-writing crusade, in establishing a new tradition. On Sunday, May 10, 1908, Miss Jarvis' mother was honored at a special service for which Anna donated 500 white carnations to be worn by everyone in attendance. From that gesture stems the custom of wearing flowers to honor one's mother. In 1914, President Woodrow Wilson proclaimed the second Sunday in May "a public expression of love and reverence for mothers of this country." In 1943, a stamp of the painting of Whistler's mother was issued as a tribute to all mothers, past and present. Today flowers and gifts, candy and cards combine with phone calls or visits home to make Mother's Day a special one for women across the land. On this day, grateful daughters and sons and husbands attempt to express their warm thoughts and thanks to mothers and wives who have meant so much.

Thought for Mother's Day

We all remember Mother
   on her special day.
We send her gifts and flowers
   and lovely cards that say
How very much we thank her
   for the things that mothers do,
The sacrifices that they make;
   but when this day is through
We're prone to take for granted
   her precious love and care,
The fact that when we need her,
   Mother's always there.
She will never mention it,
   nor ask for any praise.
The joy of doing things for us
   is her reward always.
But just the same, it would be nice,
   if we'd find time to say
Just one small word of heartfelt thanks
   to Mother—every day!

Nadine Brothers Lybarger

Thank You, Mom!

As part of their handmade Mother's Day gifts last year, the children in my youngest son's fifth grade class wrote personal letters to their moms. Along with the rest of those grade school Mother's Day presents, his letter has been carefully tucked away to become part of family folklore.

On lined paper, decorated with colored pens and with a blue ribbon at the top, David declared that "My Mother deserves the 'Mother of the Year Award' because she doesn't mind if I get my pants dirty or my shirt. And another thing is she will play poker with me till midnight. What's so neat is she doesn't mind cleaning fish. Last night we got 30 pounds of smelt and she helped! One more thing I like about my Mom is she is not scared of MICE, HAMSTERS, OR GERBILS. My mom also sometimes makes my bed and I like that."

The letter is a treasure, even though it describes my household as a rodent-infested gambling casino, smelling of fish and populated by youngsters in soiled clothing heading wearily toward their unmade beds at midnight. No pompous sentiments; no hearts-and-flowers; just a straightforward "thank-you" that only an honest ten-year-old could write.

Although his brothers are older now, and their gifts are becoming somewhat more sophisticated, they also brightened that second Sunday in May with homemade trinkets. The cardboard box in the attic holds all kinds of mementos that were drawn, colored, pasted, and stapled by little boy fingers.

One of my favorites was a cottage cheese carton, tastefully camouflaged in pastel tissue paper with a strip of construction paper for its handle. The "basket" was filled with pink and yellow flowers of unknown paper varieties, less than carefully glued to their cardboard stems. Two dozen long-stemmed roses would not have meant as much—and certainly wouldn't have lasted all these years.

David's reference to rodents was not unfounded; the animals in residence at our house (in cages) now number two gerbils named Gladys and Dolores, one black and white mouse named Cousin Gerald, and a fine, fat hamster named Albert Hendryx. Somehow I inherited the late-night feeding routine, and I report to the boys the next morning on the silly antics the little animals have staged in their delight over a handful of sunflower seeds.

So it is not surprising that one son confided to a local shopkeeper, "My mother *likes* rodents!" as he selected a dear, small china mouse as a Mother's Day gift. This same lad has provided me with my own menagerie of stuffed creatures—squirrels, rabbits, mice—and a little statue that looks something like a Tasmanian Devil.

Mink coats may come and yachts may go, but mothers understand what real treasures are: the plaster cast of a small second-grade-sized hand; the wall hanging in brilliant colors that says, simply, "Thank You, Mom!"; the booklet made out of construction paper and bound with a piece of yarn, containing pictures on each page illustrating "What My Mom Does For Me." I love the stick figure stirring a huge pot of spaghetti sauce or bending over to zip a zipper. I haven't been that thin in years.

Bea Bourgeois

I walk into my garden fair
And see the flowers blooming there;
I nestle in a shady nook
And listen to the babbling brook;   Mothers
I seem to hear the lowing herds,
The honeybees, the song of birds.

In my dreams, I onward go
To watch the sunset's golden glow;
I look into the sky at night
And see the stars shining bright;
And in the distance covering all
I see the shadow moonbeams fall.

I stand beside the ocean blue
And think of all that's good and true;
Of all the lovely things God made
There's one above all others—
He took the best from all of these
And made them into "Mothers."

Laura V. Cline

At Long Last, a Monument to Mom

Beverly Wiersum Charette

A balmy spring breeze carries the bittersweet scent of prairie flowers to the group of people gathered outside a tiny, white building. The final notes of the band's selection reverberate off the crimson, windburnished rocks nearby. Against an unparalleled backdrop of magnificent mountain peaks, some soaring to over 14,000 feet, the members of the American Mothers Committee and their honored guests, accompanied by the Air Force Academy Band, conclude their dedication of the National Mothers Chapel. On Mother's Day, May 11, 1973, a dream has become a beautiful reality.

Located in Colorado Springs, Colorado, at the foot of mountain man Zebulon Pike's namesake, this national shrine pays tribute to the mothers of America. A simple, unpretentious structure, the Chapel is visited each year by hundreds of people from all over the nation and many foreign countries. In the quiet serenity of the sanctuary, visitors can experience a moment of meditation as they view the silent majesty of God's creation—the Rocky Mountains—while, at the same time, honoring one of his greater creations—mother.

The idea of designating a national shrine to mothers formulated when Dorothy Lewis, honorary president of the American Mothers Committee, Inc., sat on the porch of her New Hampshire home, musing about the Committee's annual conference coming up in 1973. She was considering ways of maintaining the ideals of the organization in a visible way to fire the members' enthusiasm long after the conference had ended. Inspired by the beauty of the New England countryside, she conceived the notion of leaving something special in Colorado after the conference, symbolizing the organization's dedication to motherhood. It could serve, she thought, as a permanent reminder of those qualities desired in every mother, such as affection, patience, firmness, understanding, and courage. Mrs. Lewis decided that nothing could better symbolize these uniquely contrasting qualities of motherhood than a small meditation chapel surrounded by the powerful natural wonders of the Garden of the Gods and the rugged Rocky Mountains. Convinced of the need for a National Mothers Chapel, she resolved to make her vision materialize.

In the fall of 1972, Mrs. Lewis presented her plan to the members of the National Board of the American Mothers Committee.

After thoughtful deliberation, they voted to proceed with the establishment of such a monument. Committee members then embarked on a National Prayer Vigil to secure donations for its construction. Hundreds of mothers from across the country generously offered gifts, including the large picture window over the altar with its unsurpassed view of the mountains.

Thanks to the contributions of many Americans and the efforts of the American Mothers Committee, the National Mothers Chapel stands today as a symbol of motherhood, and of the whole family as well. In a time when the family unit is often threatened by the looseness of relationships, this monument is a comforting reminder of this very necessary institution.

Egypt Mother of Civilization

Henri Gougaud
Colette Gouvion
Translated from the French by Stephen Hardman

She was called Nefertiti, meaning "the most beautiful one has come," and her beauty lives on in an immortal portrait bust. Who was Nefertiti? She was the queen of the Pharoah Akhenaten of the 18th Dynasty (1373 to 1357 B.C.) and his most beloved wife. Nefertiti, love and beauty were all combined with the one god Akhenaten worshiped, Aten, the sun. A poet and visionary, the Pharoah believed in accepting the simple things of everyday life as gifts of Aten. His wife, Nefertiti, is usually depicted as a loving wife and the gentle mother of six daughters. So much did Akhenaten love his Nefertiti that her images guarded the four corners of his burial vault in the Valley of the Kings.

There are magical countries whose very names reach towards a dream world beyond the setting sun. The doorway leading to them is an invisible temple built in the mind of the traveler by mythical beings, and their last frontier post lies outside all geographical confines. Such a country is Egypt. It is bounded by a gold scarab at the threshold of the world and by a sphinx at the threshold of death; it is traversed by a fertile serpent, engendering life, and is inhabited by legend. But who gave it its roots? "A people that push the water with their feet," as the Bible says, a powerful sun in a perfect sky, a rich and majestic river, the Nile. Once the traveler has passed through the door of myth, he is confronted by water, real fire, flesh and vegetation. A first and a primary truth is established: magic Egypt is a human land.

Of a total area of nine hundred thousand square kilometers, fields and towns occupy thirty-four thousand, and barren sand and bare rock cover eight hundred and fifty-six thousand square kilometers. The population numbers thirty-six millions, nine hundred and seventy-five to the square kilometer. This is where the paradoxes begin. This country is the most empty and the most fertile, the most plentiful, the most disconcerting, the most desert-bound in North East Africa and the largest oasis in the world. Here the longest civilization of antiquity was born. Here truths contradict one another, images are piled one on another without ever losing their identity. Here the shadows have their own shadows. About 1940 a minister, Hefni Pasha, wanted to have the mirages that haunt the road from Alexandria to Cairo classified as historic monuments. He was right. In Egypt the great beauty spots are of intangible stone, history is conjugated in the past-present tense and speech navigates a course between an unreal violence and a genuine pacifism, mocking but courteous, profound but frivolous, melancholy but serene.

It is said that, three thousand two hundred years before Christ, the legendary King Menes unified the two kingdoms in a single state, the North devoted to the cult of Osiris and the South to that of the god Set. No one has ever reversed his decree. Occupying this indivisible land, however, four successive peoples have been distinguished by the geographers of the times. The Egypt of the Pharaohs asserts itself with the power of the colossi, but it remains forever as impalpable, as inaccessible as any vanished civilization. It existed for at least forty centuries—twice as long as the period dating from the dawn of Christianity. It was the mother of all the Mediterranean civilizations, of agriculture, architecture, the major techniques and arts. In short, says Ibrahim Fahri, it "invented God, the cultivation of the fava bean, secret writing and pictorial representation, the functions and habits of the soul"—life, in a word. That Egypt died, its tomb sealed by Cleopatra VII—the only known Cleopatra, loved by Caesar.

Among the temples and the gardens came strange Christians, a turbulent and scholarly body of men. At Alexandria, the favorite city of the philosophers, a crucible bubbling with ideas at this beginning of a new era, some were Gnostics, believing that study and knowledge provided a better path to God than simple faith. Others founded the Coptic Church, which was by no means militant. Today there still remain Coptic monasteries, monuments, a splendid, sensitive, sad and strangely modern art, and five million faithful.

From the end of the Roman occuption the Christians lived among the sons of Allah, who gave the East this African country where Europe soon established its influence. Muslim Egypt had its periods of excess, like every country in the world. But in the Middle Ages it was powerful, studious and refined. Its literature, passionately interested in the art of living and thinking, preserved the finest part of the Greek heritage. Its princes were great men, among them Saladin who vanquished the Crusaders. Its architects were experts: the mosques of Ibu Tulun and Hassan, the University of El Azhar were their glorious achievement. They still exert a firm hold on the heart of modern Egypt, which honors their memory and feeds on their knowledge.

Times have changed, however. This very old and venerable country was a Civilization with a capital C. Today it is a 'developing country' and of an almost impudent youthfulness: the average age of its thirty-six million inhabitants is twenty-seven, and one Egyptian in two is under twenty. Now Egypt, despite its faults and creakings, is hailed as the leading industrial nation in the Middle East and the queen of cotton. It is growing and strengthening its muscles. The Aswan dam has been built, agrarian reform organized, and the fertile lands distributed to the peasants. Wars smoulder, burst into flame and are extinguished. The population is increasing rapidly; housing is still inadequate and food is still too meager. The people still live on hope, but their hearts are strong and their souls remain strangely rich in a knowledge without words.

A moment of ordinary life is glimpsed as one passes: at the foot of the pyramids, near a fruit stall surrounded by flies, an old man is sitting on the edge of a pavement. He is dressed in a dusty *galabieh* (cotton robe) and a tattered turban. His eyes sparkle from a face riddled with lines. In the full heat of the sun he is dreaming. On the pavement opposite a tourist stops and aims his camera at him. The old man catches sight of the tourist and makes the impatient gesture of someone annoyed by an insect. The tourist insists. The man puts his hands over his face and does not budge. He refuses to be photographed, for he does not want his real face to be stolen from him and appear like a fake against a background of sky. He mistrusts images devoid of vitality.

As the traveler sets out on his journey he should think of this old man with gratitude, for he possesses a simple and precious truth: all that matters is life as it is lived. One should beware therefore of going to Egypt as if one were going to the cinema, armed with childish notions fostered by school books, Hollywood Cleopatras, colored sphinxes against a desert backdrop and museum souvenirs. And to make sure of starting with a truly open mind, forget all about any rigid preconceptions. Israel, the Arab, Suez and Port Said are newspaper words. One realizes this as soon as the first face is seen, the first look exchanged, the first word heard in the first street one sets foot on in Cairo. Egypt is first and foremost inhabited by human beings, a fact worth observing about a country where the only true ghettos are those which tourists themselves erect around their travels. So one must go and meet the real people. But do not hope to gain any clear-cut knowledge or certitude. Life is not amenable to fixed ideas. One will never force the secret of half glimpsed mysteries.

The word, however, is all powerful in Egypt. There is no other country where a greeting is so friendly, a word of love so tender, an insult so brutal, or a curse so final. The Egyptians know by instinct the exorcising power of discussion; it frees them from the need of the aggressive gesture, and, moreover, it nourishes a pacifism that is deeply rooted in their consciousness. To invest love and friendship with precious words, to insult in order not to have to fight—is this simply the Eastern way of things, or is it peculiarly Egyptian? The ancient riverside dwellers of the Nile inscribed these two sentences in hieroglyphics before the Bible existed: "The Word creates everything, all that we love and hate, the totality of being. Nothing exists before it has been uttered in a clear voice." These men possessed such powers of incantation that they made statues talk, writes Kurt Seligman in a strange book entitled *Mirror of Magic*. "The sphinxes opened their mouths of stone and revealed the will of the gods. The Fathers of the Christian Church bear explicit witness to the fact that these statues could speak. Often the king and his assembled people attended this sort of oracle, and the scribes wrote down what was said on their papyrus."

This art is lost to the world, but words still fascinate, magnifying life and filling it with a sense of wonder. "Your absence has made me wild," says the Egyptian to a returning friend—a cordial welcome in the strictest sense of the term, for the heart beats in these words. Moreover, in this country it could be said that a heart beats in all things, even in the sun which was named, blessed and implored like a god and tenderly loved like a human father, and even in the dark stone of the tombs. The sturdy peasant carved four thousand years ago on the wall of the house of a dead man, at Sakkara, can be encountered at a roadside, driving his buffaloes under the palm-trees. Along the Nile one will see women carrying pitchers of water on their heads; their exact likeness was also engraved on the wall of a temple four thousand years ago. He will discover human profiles carved on the wall of a royal tomb and will recognize them both in the university amphitheaters and among the crowds at the Ramesses station, against a background of suitcases and bundles of clothes. A child will come towards one among the oranges at the Khan el Khalili market, a crafty, chattering child, a poor child with an expression that is restless, lively, anxious, smiling, solemn, mocking, attentive and tireless. As the tourist watches him, all mirages banished, he will contemplate the indefinable reality and will finally understand these words of André Malraux: "The Egypt which first invented eternity is also the most powerful actress in life." So do not set out with the intention of discovering this country. It is Egypt which, by good fortune, will take possession of the traveler.

Extract taken from EGYPT OBSERVED by Henri Gougaud & Colette Gouvion, published by Kaye & Ward Ltd., London, England and Oxford University Press Inc., New York. First published by Librairie Hachette, Paris, France © 1976. English translation copyright © 1979 Kay & Ward Ltd.

To Young Mothers

Take time to hear their prayers at night,
   And cuddle them a little bit.
Tell them a story now and then,
   And steal a little time to sit
And listen to their childish talk,
   Or take them for a little walk.

You do not know it now—but soon
   They will be gone (the years are swift),
For life just marches on and on,
   And heaven holds no sweeter gift
Than a small boy with tousled hair,
   Who leaves his toys just anywhere.

A picnic can be such a treat,
   With sand to play in, clean and white,
When blue waves breaking on the shore
   Are filled with wonder and delight
For children armed with tins and pails
   And wooden boats with crooked sails.

Take time to laugh and sing and play,
   To really cherish and enjoy,
A little girl with flaxen curls
   And the small wonder of a boy.
They ask so little when they're small.
   Just love and tenderness—that's all.

Edna Jaques

A Gleam of Sunset Gold

The flowers are holding a gay festival this spring. The grass is as green as a rare emerald. The lilacs are waving gay plumes of fragrant lavender and cerise beauty, yes and creamy beauty, too, for all the world to see. Close by the road that leads from home, sweet home, all those who pass by can see the lovely French lilac that Mother planted when all her little flock of children were at home. Today they are scattered thousands of miles away from each other.

It seems that I can see Mother's flowers today. Yes, even so, although I see them through a mist of tears.

And not only do I envision those borders of lovely pink and red and creamy roses and the rows of the most gorgeous peonies in the world, the iris that were all the colors of the rainbow, the tulips, the hyacinths, the spirea bushes that Mother always said looked just like a sweet May bride in a cloud of white, no—not only do I hold the vision of fragrant flowers that Mother loved so well, but see the flower that I love the most in that beautiful garden, Mother. How dear she is to us all. How loyal—how true. Sacrificing so much for us. Loving us even when we sometimes hurt her. Proud of us—glorying in every achievement we accomplished. Grieving over us when we were ill or in sorrow. Precious Mother! Her faith is like the radiant stars in heaven. Her love is as deep as the sea. How brave she has been! How true and fine! Today I see her in this lovely month of May, coming in the old door of our home, arms laden with the precious French lilacs, the old-fashioned lilacs of light lavender and cream, and I hear her say as she buries her face amongst the fragrant beauties, "How I love them!" In memory I see Mother. Her brave, gallant figure out there among the flowers that she loved so well.

How can we honor our mothers enough? Today, for just one day, we wear a flower for her. Is it enough? No, it is not enough. Every day of our lives we should wear a flower for Mother. True, it may not be visible to the eye, but it can be planted deep in the tendrils of our hearts, a rose of love that grows more sweet until at last we drift upon the shores of eternity.

Mabel Reed Wilson

Masterpiece

God gave us all the wonders
Of His scenic out-of-doors,
The fresh, pure air, the bright sunshine,
Wild creatures by the score.

He carved majestic mountains
With skilled and steadfast hand;
He hollowed out the ocean's cup
And carpeted the land.

He gave us grass and trees and flowers,
Each lovely thing that grows,
The grandeur of the redwoods,
The beauty of the rose.

The rippling silver river,
The delicate snowflake,
The glory of the sunset and
The cool, blue mountain lake.

He made the stars and gave them
Each an appointed place . . .
Created then, His masterpiece,
A mother's gentle face!

Mrs. Roy L. Peifer

Mother

Mother loves the warm wind blowing
  On the far, green hill.
Mother loves geraniums growing
  At her windowsill.

Mother loves the buckwheat swaying
  In the summer breeze;
And the harvest, and the haying—
  Mother loves these!

Mother loves remembered faces,
  And old, precious things,
Mother loves brick walls and places
  Where the ivy clings.

Mother loves the upward springing
  Of the stirring sod,
And the little children singing—
  Mother loves God!

Mother loves so much that's splendid—
  Earth and reaching sky.
Many treasured joys are ended,
  Still her faith is high.

In this world where lack of loving
  Grieves us constantly,
I am glad for time's sweet proving—
  Mother loves me!

Anne Campbell

Old-Fashioned Flowers

The old-fashioned flowers seem sweetest to me,
　　For some fancied reason or other.
In each fragrant petal there's something I see
　　That always reminds me of Mother.

The mem'ry it brings me is winsomely sweet,
　　A mem'ry that never shall perish;
And in it the two of us smilingly meet,
　　A love-laden mem'ry I cherish.

We stroll through the garden, and stop here and there,
　　Admiring the colorful splendor
Of flowers she's planted and nurtured with care,
　　With hands that were loving and tender.

We stop at the roses and chat for awhile . . .
　　She tells me how sweetly they're scented,
And there midst the flowers our hearts a-smile,
　　How happy are we and contented!

And here are the zinnias, the dahlias and phlox,
　　The sunflowers, nodding and lazy;
And threading among them are neat little walks,
　　And there is an old-fashioned daisy!

And now as we're leaving the garden, I find,
　　For some fancied reason or other,
The old-fashioned flowers seem gentle and kind,
　　And so they remind me of Mother.

Charles S. Kinnison

The mother is a gardener—planting the seeds of faith,
truth and love that develop into the fairest flowers of character,
virtue and happiness in the lives of her children.

J. Harold Gwynne

The Soul of a Child

The soul of a child is the loveliest flower
That grows in the garden of God.
Its climb is from weakness to knowledge and power,
To the sky from the clay to the cloud.
To beauty and sweetness it grows under care,
Neglected, 'tis ragged and wild.
'Tis a plant that is tender, but wondrously rare,
The sweet, wistful soul of a child.

Be tender, O gardener, and give it its share
Of moisture, of warmth and of light,
And let it not lack for the painstaking care
To protect it from frost and from blight.
A glad day will come when its bloom shall unfold,
It will seem that an angel has smiled,
Reflecting a beauty and sweetness untold
In the sensitive soul of a child.

Author Unknown

Home

Home brings a vision of gardens in springtime,
Hawthorn in bloom at the side of the street,
Hedges in front where the new green is showing,
Dew on the flowers that bloom at my feet.

Cottages gray in the mists of the morning,
Daisies that peep through the green of the lawn,
Wide-open casements where roses are climbing,
Larks in the meadows and day at the dawn.

Home is a place where a mother is sitting,
Watching the road for her loved to come home,
Quiet and soft without hurry or fretting,
A place that you dream of wherever you roam.

Home means a garden with old-fashioned flowers,
Shining and clear like a welcoming star,
Clean little rooms and a chair by the fire,
Home means for me, just wherever you are.

Edna Jaques

Garden Magic

She has the gift of growing things,
The magic touch with plant and flower.
The frailest slips will grow for her,
Touched by her finger's tender power.
We asked her how she made them grow,
She laughed and said she loved them so.

Her windowsills are always gay
With blooms of every shade and hue.
She's always setting out new bulbs,
You know the way some women do.
She digs around the soil and sands,
Patting it down with loving hands.

I do not think life could bestow
A finer gift than loving toil,
The joy of helping things to grow,
Of working with the sun and soil,
That every soul you met and knew
Was lovelier, because of you.

Edna Jaques

The Story of Ruth and Naomi

We now pause in the troubled story of Israel, and for a little while listen to a romantic history which shows us something of the sweetness, gentleness, and kindness of those distant times. At this time there was peace throughout the land; but there was also a great famine.

Elimelech, with his wife Naomi, and his two sons Mahlon and Chilion, made a journey from their house to the foreign and heathen country of Moab, because of the famine. They found land and food in this strange country, and were hospitably received. Elimelech and the two sons were perfectly content with it; but Naomi sighed often for her homeland and for the company of her kinspeople.

Elimelech died, and his two sons married Moabite women. They felt themselves now thoroughly settled in the new land, and must have smiled to hear their mother Naomi constantly sighing for the land of Judah. But presently the two sons died, and poor Naomi was left alone in this foreign country, with no one to care for her but these two foreign women who had married her sons. More than ever she longed to return.

When it came to her ears that prosperity had returned to the land of Judah, the widow said that she would return to her own people. Her daughters-in-law said they would go with her, but she bade them return each to her mother's house. The two women wept, and one of them returned to her mother's house. But Ruth, the other daughter-in-law, cleaved to Naomi.

"Behold," said Naomi, "thy sister-in-law is gone back unto her people, and unto her gods: return thou after thy sister-in-law." But Ruth still clave to her, and said:

"Entreat me not to leave thee, or to return
　　from following after thee;
For whither thou goest, I will go;
　　And where thou lodgest, I will lodge;
Thy people shall be my people,
　　And thy God my God;
Where thou diest, will I die,
　　and there will I be buried;
The Lord do so to me, and more also,
　　if aught but death part thee and me."

Then Naomi loved her daughter-in-law, and the two women journeyed on together, growing in love as the miles passed behind them.

When they reached Naomi's country, the country of Israel, it was the time of barley harvest. Ruth, therefore, in order that she might get food for her mother-in-law, went to glean corn in the fields of a rich man, a relative of Naomi's dead husband.

This rich man, whose name was Boaz, saw the lovely foreign woman among the reapers, and inquired who she might be. He learned that this beautiful woman had come a long journey with her mother-in-law, even into a foreign country, and that for love of this poor mother-in-law she now gleaned among the corn to earn food and lodging. The rich and prosperous Boaz looked upon Ruth as he heard this story, and, seeing her toil there so patiently and meekly, his heart was moved with a great admiration.

So Boaz loved Ruth the Moabitess, and he made her his wife. And when a son was born to them, whose name was Obed, Naomi became nurse to it, and the family lived together in great peace and contentment. Thus was Ruth rewarded for her faithful love for her mother-in-law, and in the peace of her simple days in Israel she found joy.

But how great would her happiness have been if she had known how the child whose play she loved to watch was one day to become the father of Jesse, who was to become the father of the great David, through whom was to come the Son of Man, the Light of the World—the meek and lowly Jesus.

Harold Begbie

The Gleaners

I like to think of gentle Ruth
  As beautiful indeed,
The love of God within her heart,
  The Golden Rule her creed.

Her course was charted in a world
  So very strange and new.
But God was leading her alway—
  One of the chosen few.

Naomi begged her to return
  With Orpah, but she said
"Entreat me not to leave thee,
  But go with you instead.

"Thy God shall be my God alway,
  Thy people shall be mine."
And so to Bethlehem they went,
  This maiden so divine.

Perhaps she longed to see the land
  Her husband knew in youth.
But Naomi's heart was very glad
  For loving, trusting Ruth.

Now Boaz was a kinsman,
  A wealthy man and good,
So Ruth went forth into his field
  To glean her daily food.

And he was very pleased with her,
  As she gathered grain each day.
He showed her every kindness
  'Til the harvest was away.

Then for his wife he took her,
  And Obed was their son;
Thus, through David's generation,
  Christ's lineage was begun.

In one of the greatest dramas,
  With connecting, vital roles—
Ruth, the gleaner of barley and corn,
  And Christ, the gleaner of souls!

Ruth Ricklefs

Ruth

She stood breast-high among the corn,
  Clasped by the golden light of morn,
Like the sweetheart of the sun,
  Who many a glowing kiss had won.

On her cheek an autumn flush
  Deeply ripened, such a blush
In the midst of brown was born—
  Like red poppies grown with corn.

Round her eyes her tresses fell;
  Which were blackest none could tell.
But long lashes veiled a light
  That had else been all too bright:

And her hat with shady brim,
  Made her tressy forehead dim;
Thus she stood amid the stooks
  Praising God with sweetest looks.

Sure, I said, Heaven did not mean
  Where I reap thou should'st but glean;
Lay thy sheaf adown, and come,
  Share my harvest and my home

Thomas Hood

Courage and Crises

I have often wondered how women developed the reputation for being timid emotional creatures who can't be counted on in a crisis. American history abounds with stories of women who remained calm and decisive in any number of terrifying situations.

The simple fact is that the ingredients of this kind of courage—steady nerves, sound judgment, the ability to set aside fear—have never been exclusively masculine qualities. Nor have their opposites—panic, hysteria, and cowardice—ever been exclusively feminine.

Nevertheless, even those of us who have never accepted the popular stereotypes still feel a peculiar and perhaps inordinate sense of pride when a woman shows physical courage. Why? I used to think it was female chauvinism on my part until I realized that most men feel the same way. After further reflection, I concluded that if people make more of a fuss over feminine courage in a crisis, it is because the courage itself has an added dimension.

Ever since the days of the cavemen, males have been the acknowledged protectors of home, family, and country. It has always been assumed that they were by nature more adventurous and aggressive, more willing to risk their lives. Women, on the other hand, have had no such image to live up to. They were "the weaker sex," and it was perfectly all right for them to faint, or flee, or fail to act in a time of danger.

Thus it has been all the more surprising when a woman, who was not under any pressure to act heroically, chose to do so on her own. In almost every instance, she was going out of her way to take on a burden she could just as easily have avoided.

Commendable as this may seem to the rest of us, the women who displayed this kind of courage would probably be astonished that anyone should marvel at their actions. In the first place, most of them had neither the desire nor the temperament to play damsel in distress. More important, however, courage to them was not a question of sex or of social custom but of conscience. They had to deal with their crises courageously for one very good reason: they could not have lived with themselves if they had behaved in any other way.

Margaret Truman

Margaret Fuller

Margaret Fuller, born in Cambridge, Massachusetts, in 1810, was the daughter of a lawyer and member of the state senate. She began her education at home at the early age of four, under the supervision of her strict and disciplined father. Later, she was to become one of the brightest intellectuals and scholars of her day. Because of her early work as editor of *The Dial*, a transcendentalist magazine, she was asked to become the first woman editor of a large American newspaper, the New York *Tribune*. Her articles on women's position in society and a book on women's problems, *Woman in the Nineteenth Century*, laid the groundwork for feminism in the United States. While working as a foreign correspondent in Rome for the *Tribune*, she met her future husband, Giovanni Angelo Marquis Ossoli. They were married as war broke out in Italy. Margaret Fuller found her deepest joy and triumph in the birth of her only child, Angelo. She gave birth to her son in a quiet village outside Rome but could only rest a few days. Leaving her precious baby with a wet nurse, she resumed her correspondent duties for the *Tribune*. Returning to Rome, she sent back to America sensational, first-hand reports of the war. When foreign troops prepared to take over Rome, Margaret and Giovanni fled to the small village where they could be with their son. For a brief time they enjoyed family life. Margaret wrote of her baby, "In him I find satisfaction, for the first time, to deep wants of my heart. . . . I wake in the night—I look at him. He is so beautiful and good, I could die for him!" In 1850 she sailed with her husband and child for America. The family never reached home, their ship having been wrecked in a storm off Fire Island, New York.

Margaret Truman Daniel

Harry Truman's only daughter is best remembered for her career as a concert singer while she lived in the White House. When Truman became President in 1945, his daughter was a George Washington University co-ed who dreamed of becoming a concert singer. During her White House years Margaret resolutely continued her voice training despite public snickering. A critical review in a Washington newspaper so enraged President Truman that he wrote a blistering letter threatening to physically confront the reviewer. The letter aroused controversy, headlines, and a great deal of quiet sympathy. Now Margaret is the wife of Clifton Daniel, associate editor of *The New York Times*, and is the mother of four boys. The family lives in Manhattan, where Mrs. Daniel has found time to pursue several part-time careers: as actress, author, and host of a regularly scheduled radio interview program. Margaret Truman was not only very close to her father, but she also attentively followed his career. She has written an affectionate biography of him in which she provides some insights and asides to the official record. In recent years she has also authored another book, *Women of Courage* in which she cites examples of women who have exhibited great courage and decisiveness in times of crises.

Mary Cassatt

Mary Cassatt, born in Allegheny City, Pennsylvania, in 1845, decided at the age of seventeen that she wanted to go to Europe to study art. Her wealthy father, reluctant at first, finally consented after she had spent four unrewarding years at the Pennsylvania Academy of Fine Arts. She stayed in Paris more than three years, attending art classes until she was forced to return home during the Franco-Prussian War. While she was visiting friends in Chicago, most of her paintings were destroyed in the Chicago fire. Determined to start again, she sailed for Italy where she was greatly inspired by studying the old Italian master Correggio. Her first painting, *On the Balcony,* was accepted at the Paris Salon, an annual European exhibit. Eventually, members of her family came over to live with her, and she began what was to be a lifelong habit: using them as models. Over the next years her work was influenced by Velasquez, Rubens, the Impressionists, particularly Degas, and by Japanese art. During the 1890s she turned to the theme for which she is most noted: mother and child studies. She never married and remained childless, yet no artist has ever painted the relationship of mother and child with such tender inventiveness. She posed children carefully, thoughtful of their comfort, using mostly the local French peasant children. Charming or plain, she painted them just as they were. The Paris press was to comment on the "family life painted with distinction and love." Progressive blindness stopped all her work in 1914. By the time of her death in 1926, she was recognized as the outstanding American painter of the nineteenth century.

Lillian Gilbreth

Lillian Gilbreth was born in Oakland, California, in 1878 into a well-to-do, close-knit family. At the University of California she excelled, especially in English and psychology, and later did postgraduate work at Columbia University in New York City. She married Frank Gilbreth, an established contractor, in 1904. Gilbreth told his wife that he wanted her to be a partner in his work, just as he would be a partner in raising the family. From that point on the Gilbreths worked together as industrial engineers and became innovators, incorporating the findings of psychology into industrial research. They were also pioneers in the attempt to eliminate useless motions in industry and in the home. Their home became their laboratory-workshop and business office. Almost from babyhood their twelve children, six boys and six girls, learned how to keep the extra-large household running easily. Lillian Gilbreth's focal role in this household is described by two of her children, Frank and Ernestine, in their book *Cheaper by the Dozen*: "Mother had her first half-dozen babies at home, instead of in hospitals, because she liked to run the house and help Dad with his work. . . . The house ran smoothly by itself during the one day devoted to the delivery." When Frank Gilbreth died in 1924, Lillian continued the couple's work, receiving numerous honors and awards. She remained active, lecturing around the world, until her death in 1972.

Margaret Mead

The combination of marriage and work as a creative union was very much a part of the upbringing of Margaret Mead. Her father was a professor of economics and her mother a social scientist. Margaret was born in Philadelphia in 1901, the oldest child in her family. In college, she majored in psychology, while becoming increasingly interested in the field of anthropology, which she later pursued in postgraduate work. She was one of the first anthropologists to go directly to existing primitive cultures and bring back eyewitness reports. Her first field trip was to Samoa where she studied the adolescent girls of that culture. She found that her being a woman was an asset in that she could live in the home group and come close to the young girls and their mothers. She later made field trips to New Guinea and Bali. Her research studies, published in a succession of popular books, brought her recognition as one of the most distinguished scholars and social scientists of this century. She bore one daughter, Mary Catherine, during her marriage to English anthropologist Gregory Bateson. Margaret organized her family life by a sort of communal adjustment whereby the Bateson's moved in with friends who themselves had six children. The two families made a lively and congenial group. In recent years before her death in 1978, Dr. Mead served as curator of ethnology at the American Museum of Natural History, while continuing to make profound contributions to American society.

Two Kinds of Feeling

Often, as a mother bathes, feeds, and dresses her child, her face expresses two kinds of feeling that seem contradictory to the child and to the bystander. There is the look of unconditional devotion and blind pride in this, her child, and at the same time a look of anxious appraisal as she holds the infant away from her breast or watches the toddler's first stumbling steps and rocking gait.

For the child must go forth from the warmth and safety of its mother's care—first to take a few steps across the room, then to join playmates, and later to go to school, to work, to experience courtship and marriage, and to establish a new home. A boy must learn how different he is from his mother; he must learn that his life is turned outward to the world. A girl must learn, as she walks beside her mother, that she is both like her mother and a person in her own right. It is one of the basic complications of a mother's life that she must teach one thing to her sons and other things to her daughters.

Some peoples emphasize the mother's task more than the child's; they say that it is the mother, not the child, who is weaned. But all peoples, however differently they phrase the mystery of conception and provide for the care and safety of the mother and the child at birth, make provision—some well and others in a blundering way—for this double aspect of motherhood. All peoples build into their conception of the relationship of mother and child the care that must continue and the slowly awakening recognition that these are two persons—at birth, at physical weaning, at the child's first step, and at the child's first word that allows the child to call from a distance. And as the child lets go of its mother's hand, [it is] sure that it can return to be fed and rocked and comforted. . . .

On this unbroken continuity, on this ebb and flow of feeling between the child and the mothering woman, depends the child's sense of being a whole, continuing person—the same person today, yesterday, and tomorrow, the same person tired or rested, hungry or satiated, sleepy or wakeful, adventurous or quietly contented.

Margaret Mead

The Picture of Mother

Thomas P. Carey

I keep a priceless painting embedded in my heart,
A gift to me from heaven in the Master's perfect art;
A little homelike picture of a mother, oh, so dear,
Whose prayers I fondly cherish, and whose lessons I revere.

No vision so poetic could the brush of man portray,
The works of loving kindness must be wrought in God's own way;
Many thoughts I lend in fancy, and how true it seems to be,
The earth must have its angels, and this one abides with me.

Her hair is winter whitened and her eyes are summer blue,
Like clouds of snowy softness when the sunbeams trickle through;
Her handclasp sometimes trembles and a halting step occurs,
But oh, the tender sweetness of that patient soul of hers.

And more and more this picture is to me a sacred shrine;
I praise the God who gave it, and I thank Him that 'tis mine;
And the sun and stars may perish, and the world may fall apart,
But Mother lives forever, embedded in my heart.

From Gibson Girls to Postwar Curls

Elias Howe's invention of the sewing machine, patented in 1846, democratized fashion by giving birth to the ready-to-wear industry. Manufacturers quickly began to produce low-cost copies of the latest designs. Once, only women wealthy enough to afford dressmakers could follow fashion's whims. Now, anyone from a schoolteacher to a maid servant could wear low-cost facsimiles of the exotic creations current in Paris. From about 1860 on, thanks to pattern makers like Ellen Demorest, a woman could sew even stylish gowns on her home sewing machine.

Not everyone, however, liked the new democracy. *Vogue*, the arbiter of fashion, wrote: "The greatest lesson our women have to learn is to dress according to their position in life. If they have not great fortunes summing up to millions, why follow suit with a woman who has?" Needless to say, the newly fashionable class paid little heed to *Vogue's* admonition.

The Gibson Girl

Born in the drawings of Charles Dana Gibson, the Gibson Girl was the quintessential figure of the Gay Nineties. She dressed in a shirtwaist ensemble: a gathered skirt and high-necked, lace-trimmed blouse with long, mutton-chop sleeves. Hardly an inch of her costume lacked some sort of decoration. Though the bustle had gone the way of hoops and overblown petticoats, whalebone corsets still determined part of the female contour. Figures were tugged into the hourglass shape, an exaggerated conception of the female form best exemplified by actress Lillian Russell. The ideal woman of the era was no longer dainty and plump, but tall and willowy. Her hair was caught up in a tall, loose pompadour, whose height was achieved by backcombing or pinning hair over small rolls of lamb's wool called "rats."

Early feminist Elizabeth Cady Stanton once said, "Many a woman is riding to suffrage on a bicycle." Likewise, the bicycle fad of the late nineteenth century did much to liberate women's fashions. Though Ellen Penrose was arrested at Coney Island in 1887 for wearing bloomers while bicycling, they and knickerbockers were considered proper attire for female bikers by the turn of the century. "To wheel far, one must breathe," cautioned an opponent of corsets and tight clothes for bicyclers at an 1896 meeting of the New York Academy of Medicine.

Goodbye Child, Hello Woman

After one last outburst of Victoriana, the first half of the twentieth century saw an almost continual pruning of the Gibson Girl silhouette.

The Art Deco period and the popularity of the streamlined, curvilinear design opened the century. The 1910 woman dressed up in floor-length, low-necked columns of silk and wool embellished with finely hand-sewn details. Her accessories were likewise streamlined: stoles, long necklaces, trailing silk scarves, and handbags suspended by long cord handles. Her hats were wide brimmed, heavily plumed, and frequently veiled. (When automobiles replaced carriages, dustcoats as well as veils came into vogue, more because they were practical than fashionable.) Fashions, like the women who wore them, were becoming more worldly.

For everyday wear, tailored ready-to-wear ensembles were popular. Such suits were pared-down versions of the Gibson Girl's shirtwaist, minus ruffles, pleats, trains, and other fluff. Skirt lengths had just begun their ascent, hovering in the vicinity of the ankle. Though the whalebone corset was gone, woman's freedom of movement was still limited by her long, narrow "hobble skirt."

As new modes of transportation and communication shrank the globe, fashion changed more quickly than ever. Despite increasingly swift production, a new look was often old by the time it reached ready-to-wear stores in the far reaches of the United States.

As the theater, and soon the movies, gained respectability, the influence of theatrical costume design increased. For example, the motif of Lev Bakst's costumes for *Scheherazade* turned up in the sashes, fringes, braiding, and strong colors of 1914 street wear and negligees.

Makeup was in accepted, if subtle, use. A woman could choose cosmetics from the offerings of Yardley, Helena Rubinstein, or Cheeseborough-Ponds, much as she might today. Her hair was still long, most often swept back into a knot.

Flapping to the Speakeasy

The 1920s began quietly enough with a post-war dip in skirt lengths. But by 1925, things were roaring. Skirts rose steadily, from mid-calf in 1920 to the knee several years later. Corsets flattened the natural curves and obliterated any hint of a waistline, creating a boyish silhouette compatible with the low- or no-waisted garments then in fashion. The flapper didn't care for the full, loose styles and staid colors her older sister had chosen in 1920. She preferred a daring sleeveless chemise with boat neck, a beaded geometric pattern on the bodice, and pleated flounce from hip to knee. She might also have owned a dress with a handkerchief hemline, or a two-piece jersey suit topped by a cardigan jacket such as that introduced by Gabrielle "Coco" Chanel. Silk stockings became an important accessory as more of the leg was shown.

Like Irene Castle and Clara Bow, the flapper bobbed her hair and combed it flat against her head. A deep-crowned cloche, adorned at most with a feather or bow, hugged her head. The obviously painted face was now popular. The flapper liberally applied rouge, powder, and mascara. She painted her lips into a bright red cupid's bow.

Jaded Elegance

The 1930s woman projected a more mature image. Unlike the frenetic flapper, she was coolly sophisticated —sometimes even jaded. The Great Depression that followed the stock market crash of 1929 was not an era for conspicuous grandeur; fashion elegance was in the cut and hang of a garment rather than in lavish embellishments.

Women of the early thirties wore clinging, bias-cut dresses of crepe, jersey, and rayon. (Synthetic textiles had been available since the end of World War I.) Neutral colors regained popularity and skirts fell abruptly to mid-calf. V-necklines, collared and accented with a brooch or artificial flower, came into vogue. Cap sleeves were seen along with long, tight ones. The college girl look—skirts, sweaters, and blouses—gave limited wardrobes mix-and-match flexibility.

By the mid-thirties, the clingy dress had been replaced by an updated tailored suit with a narrow skirt and close-fitting jacket. For day, the suit was made of linen or wool; for evening, it was velvet or lamé with appliqué or sequin decorations. Hems moved upward along with the nation's economy. Women began to wear trousers on the golf course—but not yet on the street, unless the woman was Katharine Hepburn.

Woman often emulated the look of their favorite screen stars: Greta Garbo's trench coat and slouch hat, Jean Harlow's halter-necked satin evening gown, and Joan Crawford's padded shoulders were frequently copied.

The flat, linear look in female bodies remained fashionable throughout the thirties. Woman wore corsets or the new one-piece foundation garment to minimize bust and hips.

Shoes, sometimes with platform heels, received much attention from designers of the thirties, low-heeled sports oxfords, "barefoot" sandals with ankle straps, t-straps, and suede pumps were popular styles.

The face of the thirties had pale cheeks, thin-plucked eyebrows, and deep red or burgundy lips. Nails, too, were painted. The hair was Harlow's: longer, freer, and platinum blonde. Popular hats were the beanie, the draped turban, and the "halo hat" with turned-up brim.

Wartime Austerity

Fashions had to be simple during World War II; U.S. law limited the number of yards of fabric used in clothing. Many French fashion houses closed during the German occupation, and imports from those that remained open were banned.

The tailored shirtwaist dress with A-line skirt was the standard costume of the woman who went to work during World War II. Skirts had risen to knee level. Influenced by the military uniforms of their men, women sprouted wider shoulders with the help of triangular pads of fabric pinned or sewn inside their dresses. A version of the waist-length, patch-pocketed battle jacket worn by General Dwight D. Eisenhower appeared on many American women. Trousers, belted and pleated at the waist, had finally become acceptable for casual wear.

With the advent of pancake makeup in 1938, the suntanned look was in. Women combed their hair up into pompadours or wore their curls long and loose a la Rita Hayworth.

Back to Femininity

With the war over, men returned to the workplace. Women returned to the home—and to restrictively feminine fashions. Christian Dior more than made up for wartime yardage restrictions in 1947 with his "New Look": longer, fuller skirts, cinched waists, rounded soft shoulders, petticoats, and corsets. Hems plunged to no more than eight inches off the floor. Shoes had high heels and pointed toes. Nylon stockings appeared on the market for the first time. In terms of comfort and convenience, the New Look was a regression into the old idea that women's clothing should be pretty, even if impractical.

The sheath dress and stiletto heels of the early fifties insured that women would continue walking "like ladies." The sheath, often made in a knitted material, fell straight from the shoulders and was belted at the waist. Every fashionable woman's wardrobe included a "little black dress," short white gloves, bandeau hat (almost always veiled), and two-tone patent leather or black suede heels.

Few popular fashions have had only one life. The last decade has seen revivals of twenties bobbed hair, thirties platform sandals, forties shoulder pads, and fifties strapless gowns. Even Turkish trousers, an updated version of 1841's shocking bloomers, were born again in the seventies. Little wonder antique clothing stores are doing a booming business.

These pages from THE GOOD HOUSEKEEPING WOMAN'S ALMANAC, copyright © 1977 by Newspaper Enterprise Association, Inc., New York, N.Y.

Always Lilacs and Fruit Jars

The spring had been wet and cold. Most of the usual flowers were long delayed in blooming; very little color could be seen in the big, old-fashioned yard.

It was almost Decoration Day. What would we do? As usual, our mom had the answer.

"Why, there are always lilacs."

It was true. We had several big bushes in our yard, even then filling the air with their fragrance. Great branches could be taken from them, and still they would have blooms to spare.

"But what will we put them in?"

Mom smiled. "Fruit jars, of course." She showed us how to break long stems with the flowers, carefully wrap them in wet newspaper for the long journey to the cemeteries, then fill the fruit jars with water when we arrived.

Always lilacs and fruit jars. Year after year. Some years there were also snowballs, even a few early, hardy roses. But always there were lilacs, great purple sprays of bursting buds.

Some of my earliest childhood memories are centered around Decoration Day, as it was called then. Not only was it a Memorial Day for military heroes, it was a day of honor and respect for all those who had lived their lives courageously, fought the good fight and triumphantly marched on. There was nothing sad or morbid about it; it was a time of joy, a time of meeting relatives both present and past.

Our first stop was the cemetery in our own little town. Here were many of Dad's and Mom's family. Many of them had been gone before we children were ever born, but they were no strangers to us! In a world without television or movies, we had been told and retold all the exciting tales of these pioneer people who had come to the Northwest just after the turn of the century and carved a home from the wilderness. They were real, alive, and it was with happiness we sought out their marking stones to put down our offerings . . . of lilacs in fruit jars.

It was a two- or three-hour drive to the larger town some fifty miles away. The cemetery there was bigger, a little more formal, yet it too was a place to find those we knew of and had learned to love. There we also met many living relatives and friends, all bound for the same goals. Many of them brought flowers. It was a little more temperate climate, not so close to the mountains—but they, too, had lilacs in fruit jars. When all the graves had been decorated, all the former family members "visited," it was time to go home with those who lived nearby. We always had a potluck dinner and spent the afternoon before climbing back into our old car for the long trip home over washboardy roads that had never known the touch of paving.

Decoration Day. A day of giving tribute. A day of joy and remembering. Through the years it has become Memorial Day. Yet somehow, it isn't quite the same.

Today I wander through the beautiful cemeteries, looking at markers ornate and simple, large and small. There are beautiful floral pieces, some real, some artificial. There are roses, and lilies, and all the wonderful flowers that can be grown in a greenhouse, in costly vases.

But very seldom now do I find lilacs grown in an old-fashioned yard, and even less often is there a plain fruit jar to hold the water, keeping the humble bouquet damp and fresh for at least a few days.

Always lilacs and fruit jars. In some strange, unexplainable way they not only tie me to my childhood, but they tie me to all those who have gone before. With the perfume of lilacs I remember the stories of Daddy Towne, who went to a tiny mountain village containing one little grocery store and even saloons and built a community church. I remember Granddad Fortner, with his patriarchal bearing, his God-fearing family, his many children. I remember Pap-Pap, my own grandfather, with his white mustache and kindly face. I remember my great-uncle Mark, who lived about a quarter mile from us out in the country. He had a bear trap cage on wheels which he hauled high up on the mountain. When a bear was in the cage, Uncle Mark would go after it with the wagon, put it in the huge backyard cage he had built, keep it for about a year and feed it on corn, then turn it into winter's meat.

I remember the Little Grandma, who, only five feet tall, stood beside her over-six-foot husband, supporting him in his endeavors.

And still more and more, family I had known in person, family I had known only through the loving eyes of my parents. Decoration Day was for them all.

It was a time to take stock of ourselves, too, to know that because of our heritage, something was expected of us. We had been given a standard to live by. From the time we were tiny we were taught that.

I wonder today how many of those who visit their families on Memorial Day have the privilege we did, of knowing and loving so many ancestors. In this hustle-bustle world, do parents still have or take time to share with children those who "broke trail" for us? I hope so. For children have the right to love and cherish their ancestors, even those they have never met. And so long as the world goes on, homage can be paid—even if only with lilacs and fruit jars.

Colleen L. Reece

A Mother's Prayer

I thank thee, Lord in Heaven above,
For giving me a baby's love,
Those precious arms that hold me tight,
Those soft, warm lips that kiss good night,
That baby chatter, soft and sweet,
The patter of those tiny feet.

I thank you for that love so true,
Those sparkling eyes like shining dew,
That silken hair, that tiny nose,
Those cheeks like petals on a rose,
That grin that takes my breath away
And makes me love him more each day.

I thank you for that precious smile,
That seems contagious afterwhile,
And when I tuck him in his bed,
And gently kiss his curly head,
Only a mother's heart can know,
What makes me love my baby so.

I thank you for his loving ways,
His baby laughter through the days,
Those teeth of pearl, that heart of gold,
Please guide his steps as he grows old,
And help me, Lord, to worthy be
Of such responsibility.

Stella Wagner

A ROYAL ART REVISITED

Tatting, the genteel art of making fine lace with a shuttle, almost got lost in the rush of the twentieth century. In great-grandmother's day it was the rage. Ladies tatted because they looked so graceful at the work and because they needed beautiful laces to trim their ornate dresses and edge their linens.

Even into the 1950s women's handwork magazines carried tatting designs, but the popularity of the lace died out with the last generation of great-grandmothers. Volumes on tatting have become rare books. You'll find them listed as such in public libraries, but you'll also find, if you go to read them, that many are missing—stolen.

With the resurgence of interest in handwork, particularly macramé, women and a few bold men are again turning to tatting, but there is little material available to the beginner who doesn't resort to stealing. Most needlework encyclopedias still include a token chapter on the subject, but these are not particularly helpful. One of the most complete handbooks on the market is candid about it. In the introduction the writer admits, "The technique [of tatting] is somewhat difficult to describe. If you do not know how to tat and would like to learn, try to augment the information in this chapter with a lesson or two from a friend who knows the art." The problem is that friends like that are one in a million.

But tatting is not difficult. There is only one stitch to master, actually two half hitches, which form a common seaman's knot. The word *tatting,* itself, comes from the French *tater,* to touch. "It does not need thought or counting and is ideal to pick up in a moment's leisure," an old book on the subject notes.

Some researchers will tell you that early Egyptians discovered tatting, while others credit the Chinese or the Italians. The idea had, no doubt, been around for centuries, when it came into vogue as a simple and inexpensive means of imitating fine laces. By the 1700s, however, European nobility had taken up the art—and certainly not for thrift.

During this period tatting was often referred to as "knotting," especially by the English, and indeed, it was not tatting as we know it today. As yet no one had devised a means of joining individual tatted rings, which left the work loosely structured, dependent on being sewed down.

The problem was solved in the mid-1800s, with one Mlle. Eleanore, Riego de la Branchardiere taking credit. Mlle. Riego de la B. was the first to join tatted rings by means of the decorative loops (She called them pearls, we call them picots.) that surround them, and her designs were widely purchased in book series. Tatting became even more popular, and there were more refinements. Since tatted lace now had body and no longer needed to be sewn together, finer threads could be used and smaller shuttles were developed, often with a pointed pick or hook to facilitate joining.

Tatting remained popular until World War I. Handbooks of that era show directions for dress tops, bedspreads, tablecloths, antimacassars, and even window-shade pulls. But through the war years, dress became simpler and so did our lifestyle. We cut down on the trimmings.

The French call tatting *frivolité,* which also translates "frivolous or trivial," and so it may seem. One can use only so many fine lace collars, and edged handkerchiefs are reserved nowadays mostly for weddings. Yet tatting is unusually strong and durable. Far more so than ordinary lace or crochet, which unravels easily. It also takes less concentration than many handcrafts and is less awkward to manage on airplanes and in waiting rooms.

Taking these things into consideration, and being a dedicated tatter who enjoys the work, I began finding practical uses for the art. I hate lace-trimmed sheets. Antimacassars won't stay on plastic blow-up chairs or leather couches. And I don't have any window shades that need lace pulls. But I do love feminine clothing, bright wall hangings, and colorful trim.

Traditionally, tatting has been limited to fine threads, mostly whites and pastels, but for no good reason. If the Queen of Romania could tat gold wire, I decided, I could tat dyed hemp.

Dyed hemp, of course, won't fit on the conventional tatting shuttle, but that didn't prove a problem. I found I could work it with a Norwegian fishnet needle and, later, with a simple shuttle of my own manufacture, which I've modestly named the Morgan Shuttle.

Lael Morgan

Something for Mother

Let's go antiquing!
It's that kind of day.
A warm April sun
Chased the storm clouds away.
Let's hop on the Flyer—
Take the suburban bus.
Something for Mother
Is just waiting for us.

Surrounded at last
By bell, book and candle,
Things to be touched or
Marked "Do not handle,"
Through sliding glass doors
Or out on the lawn,
Collectibles nestle while
Their mem'ries live on.

Smell all that dust,
Although some things are polished.
Imagine the antiques
Our family demolished.
See that Grandfather's clock,
Stone barrels for pickles,
Racks and glass shelves
Filled with pennies and nickles.

These walls seem to scowl
Through dust-glinted frames.
Portraits of unknowns—
Forgotten last names.
This sweet china doll
Was once known as Molly.
See the lithos and prints
By Picasso and Dali.

Ankle length aprons and
Little white caps
Remind me of Grandma
And her afternoon naps.
See the copper utensils—
A teakettle, too,
Cauldrons for steaming
A fine Irish stew.

Springerle molds and
Oak chopping boards.
Rings made of bronze
Cut from samurai swords.
Medicine bottles to
Wear on the belt,
Guest towels, leather goods,
Bags made of felt.

Oh, those hand-engraved goblets
That fine cobbler's last.
Quilts made of velvet
With scenes from the past.
Wedgewood and Spode—
Bright Chinese prints,
And a butcher's block table
With smooth curving dents.

It's time to have lunch
At Ye Olde Parson's Bench.
Some heavenly food
Makes antiquing a cinch.
Can't wait to show you
My gold scarab ring.
But please, never ask
What I paid for the thing.

Do you like this old painting?
The frame is a mess.
It was back in a corner—
The junk room, I guess.
Mom will just love it.
It isn't too mod.
And I know in my heart
It's a Mary Cassatt.

Alice Leedy Mason

Dreams of the Heart

Ruth B. Field

Under the silver needle grows
Beauty in color, charming gay.
The art of stitchery softly glows
In flowers and forms in fair array.

Here are the blossoms of the field,
Children and animals captured there.
Carefully, then, the needle wield
Creating beauty with infinite care.

Rainbow shades and brown and green,
Beast and bud and birds and bloom,
All stitched into a charming scene,
Lovely as on Mother Nature's loom.

Stitchery portrays dreams of the heart.
Lovingly grows each scene benign,
Weaving the new or ancient art
Into a pattern of life's design.

MOTHER PLAYS HER ROLE

Excerpt from *Life with Mother and Father*
by Clarence Day

Mother had a strong and instinctive desire to play her role to the full. If she had been the queen of a court, she'd have started right in being regal and gracious, stirring up the lord chamberlain, and making sure the king toed the mark. Anything that it was customary for an energetic queen to attend to, Mother would have at once had a go at. So just as soon as Father had laid out the grounds of his new home in the country, and Mother could see that there was something more to it than a lot of mess and workmen, she christened the place Upland Farm and determined to fill a useful role there.

She was handicapped because she really didn't know anything about farms or farming. As to the proper method of growing crops in a field, that was a mystery to her, and anyhow it was a man's job. Even our vegetable garden was too large a problem for her to tackle. What she liked to do was to grow flowers in little pots on the piazza. This came to be a department in itself, she had so many pots, and they all had to be watered. On hot summer nights after the gardener had finished his other work, we would hear his unwilling footsteps around the corner of the house as he came to fill the big watering can at the faucet near the steps. However, if there was a drought, the gardener said these plants were not important. Mother would then bestir herself to preserve their lives by taking water out to them herself.

Though this was interesting enough as an occupation, it did not give her a role. Of course there was the moving back and forth—and Mother felt no one understood the magnitude of this task—but it was an exceptional thing that only overtook one twice a year. And most of the impending catastrophes were avoided anyway. When Father discovered that the jar of preserved strawberries had been packed with the tea and his cheese in a wash boiler with many other articles, and remonstrated, Mother knew of so many more dangerous packages than the strawberries that she brushed him aside with the remark that as nothing had happened to anything, why was he making all this talk.

However, almost any situation has a role in it for a wide-awake woman, and Mother finally found hers through prodding Father and the farmer to make Upland Farm more and more farmlike, so that the name would seem right and fitting to others. Of course the very first year there had been a kitchen garden, but it wasn't enough for her to serve vegetables from our garden at dinner, and tell her guests triumphantly that the peas had come right out of our own pea patch, and promise to march them down after dessert and show them the beans, too, and the place where the melons

were to have been if they hadn't all dried up in infancy. This sort of thing didn't content her, because we didn't have enough guests.

We boys benefited at first from her extension of the production of vegetables because we used to take all that we could lay our hands on and drive off in the farm cart and sell them. This opportunity to earn money so easily made up in part to us for our former summers at New London; but it was not destined to last, for we found before long that there did not seem to be so many vegetables that wouldn't be missed. We also discovered that our market was being spoiled, for we soon noticed that Mother would go out in the victoria, dressed in her fresh, ruffled dresses, and holding her lace parasol so as to shade her face, and make calls on her friends in the afternoon. With her she would carry a basket of vegetables to those who had no garden of their own, or, to the more fortunate, something not to be found in their garden. The next morning when four red-headed and freckled boys drove up to sell their vegetables, all the houses would be mysteriously stocked.

But it was the cows who gave Mother her first real responsibility in her role of chatelaine. At first there had been only one cow, but there had come a time when she went dry. In order to avoid any such stoppage of our milk supply, the next year a second cow had been added; as the years went on, more cows were about the place. Father bought a fancy one to improve the stock, or kept a heifer, until finally there were always five.

When we first settled there, Harrison was out in the country, but little by little it became a suburb. The farms, old and new, disappeared. Even the parklike estates were split up into smaller holdings or turned into clubs. Almost none of our neighbors had barns or kept cows any more. It was easier to buy milk and butter. Mother didn't like to depend on bottled milk, though, and as she also was proud of our butter, she clung to all our cows.

Father and Mother had no use for five cows, especially when the time came that they were alone on the place; but by that time each of the cows had become a member of the family, even the two cranky ones and the stupid old white one which none of us liked.

For a while it was a problem to get the milk down daily to the city for the family's use during the winter. Express companies, while willing to take on the order, did not feel they had to be at our house at any appointed hour to deliver a can of milk. Mother, who had to deal with the cook, felt strongly they should be. Certainly the time for milk to come to any house was early in the morning. Everybody knew that.

However, right near the Grand Central station was a grocery store the family had used for years, a comfortable, established firm. There they mixed Father's coffee just to his taste, and saw to it that his cigars were right. As the station checking system for parcels was not as well arranged then as now, old customers left their bundles behind the grocery-store counters to be called for later in the day. I can't remember how or why, but we once left a grandfather's clock there for over a year. The name of this long-suffering grocer was Charles.

Since the store was so near the station, Mother felt that it would be no trouble at all to them to have a man run over and get our can of milk off the train from Harrison and send it up to the house with the first delivery. Perhaps it was because the family had traded for a long time with them, or perhaps because they had been accustomed for an equally long time to Mother's and Father's difficult requests; at any rate, they consented to do this. The arrangement worked very well for us, but if Charles' was so unfortunate as to be only half an hour late in delivering the can, they were called right up and scolded roundly. If the farmer did not put the can on the usual train, or if it was delayed, Charles' found themselves not only apologizing but anxiously meeting each train from Harrison until the milk arrived. They would then send a man straight up to our house on a special trip with the can.

Meanwhile the cows gave milk—more milk than the family knew what to do with. The farmer and the coachman and their children and wives were chock-full of it. So were the chickens and the pigs. Moreover, Mother did not play her part—she lived it, and she insisted that all the milk be set for cream. This meant that in summer the cream became pretty sour by the time the farmer got around to churning a large part of it into butter. None of us thought of complaining about the taste of the butter, except one of my brothers, who always loathed it.

When the family got smaller, we not only had too much butter, but the house was drowned in cream. Great bowls and pitcherfuls would come on the table. Mother, knowing about all the cream down in the dairy waiting to be churned, would wearily order any cream that was left after luncheon to be brought out on the porch. There she would sit on a broiling hot day whipping it into butter. Sometimes the butter was obstinate and Mother would have to leave it while she went and changed her dress so as to be ready for callers in the afternoon. On those days, when visitors drove up they would find Mother sitting there in her chair still beating away.

There were two things about our butter that prevented it from being really good. One was that Father had started out with the best of pedigreed Jersey stock. This strain of cow gives delicious, rich milk and cream, but the butter has a strong taste. The second was that our farmer never washed the butter sufficiently to take all

of the buttermilk out of it. The color, however, was always beautiful, and both Mother and the farmer took great pride in never having to use any artificial coloring matter to give it that rich, golden look.

By the time the family had been reduced to just Mother and Father and they had grown old and had fewer and fewer guests, Mother found that the butter was not only a responsibility but a real problem. Some of it she gave away to friends who were sick or poor. There were one or two families, however, who were rich and who, Mother felt, could well afford to buy themselves nice, fresh, country butter. I don't know whether they really intended to do so, but at any rate they did buy our butter. And Mother was very particular that these orders should never fail to be delivered. When she returned to town from her weekly trips to the country, one of the most precious articles she carried with her was a large stone crock which was placed in the car last, because on the way home the chauffeur would have to stop at Mrs. Dickerman's and walk up to the door, bearing in his arms, patiently or disdainfully according to the nature of the chauffeur, this large earthenware crock full of round pats of butter. If these friends did not like the butter, they never said so; therefore Mother continued to be serene about bestowing it as a special privilege.

Once, some especially bankerish and well-tailored people came to dine. They were English friends of my brother who had never liked the butter. They innocently asked if there was anything they could take back to England, where he was now living, in the country. Mother was equal to any emergency of that variety and instantly took them up on this offer.

The day they sailed home Mother stopped in to see me at my apartment in town and spoke of how kind they were.

"What did you send?" I asked.

"Why," said Mother, "I sent him some of the farm butter."

I had seen these people; tall, slim, elegant. They had no wrinkles in their clothes and their manners were studied and quiet. I had a quick vision of their carrying something rather bulkily wrapped in brown paper, for Mother, although she dearly loved to do up parcels, had never the patience to make them come out just right. I hoped that they would be able to get it from the ship's refrigerator to my brother quickly, so that no tell-tale grease spots would greet my brother's eye as he put out his hand to receive this gift.

"Don't you think you might have sent something else?" I asked. "They rather specialize in fresh butter over there."

"But not our butter from Harrison," Mother proudly answered.

On the following six pages
we are presenting a selection
from Mother's Ideals, 1947.

Mother's

ideals

(VOL. 2)

Star of My Life

Even before I breathed the breath of life,
Your prayers, like rays of heavenly light,
Illumined safe paths for me to tread,
To point my ways in places bright.
Through childhood days of helplessness
And mystery, strange pain and tears,
You led me ever from the depths
Of joyless hours, from needs or fears:
Star of my life—My Mother.

New interests with added years
Have come, but none that does imbue
With greater faith than your sure love;
No orb that gleams more brightly through
The clouds that float across my view
To peace and happiness and God,
To guide, to comfort, to sustain,
As life's uneven course I plod:
Star of my life—My Mother.

I know 'tis not without distress
You've kept your light before my feet;
Oft times I've followed errant bent
And brought you grief and sore defeat.
But your true life and patient love
Have e'er kept plain the surer way.
Though I fall short, you have not failed;
For this I honor you today:
Star of my life—My Mother.

Our sincere thanks to the unknown author whose
address we were unable to locate.

Full-Fashioned Mother

By Ruby Wayburn Tobias

My mother did not have the placid gaze
Madonnas wear, but in a dozen ways
She made me think of them — her playful
    air
That almost camouflaged her constant care;
The blue-checked apron where we wiped our
    tears,
And often, little telltale cooky smears;
The smell of fresh-baked bread, and potted
    bloom
Of heliotrope she kept for her perfume;
The limp in one brave foot that couldn't
    quite
Keep up with youngsters eager for a flight;
Her brief sharp scolds and all the tender fuss
That somehow kept in bounds the five of us;
Her snatchy songs, her stories and her
    prayers,
The meted tasks that shaped us unawares —

My mother! You may say, "How common-
    place!"
You may not see Madonnas in her face.
But anyway, those blue-checked apron
    strings
Are my conception of an angel's wings.

Our sincere thanks to the author whose
address we were unable to locate.

Our Mother

Author Unknown

How oft some passing word will tend
In visions to recall
Our truest, dearest, fondest friend —
That earliest friend of all.

Who tended on our childish years,
Those years that pass as hours,
When all earth's dewy, trembling tears,
Lie hid within her flowers.

The star that shines in darkest night,
When most we need thy aid,
Nor changes but to beam more bright
When others coldly fade.

Oh, mother! round thy hallowed name
Such blissful memory springs,
The heart in all but years the same,
With reverent worship clings.

Thy voice was first to greet us, when
Bright fortune smiling o'er us,
And thine hand that's readiest then
To lift the veil before us.

Or if dark clouds close round our head
And care steals o'er the brow,
While hope's fair flowers fall crushed and dead
Unchanged still art thou.

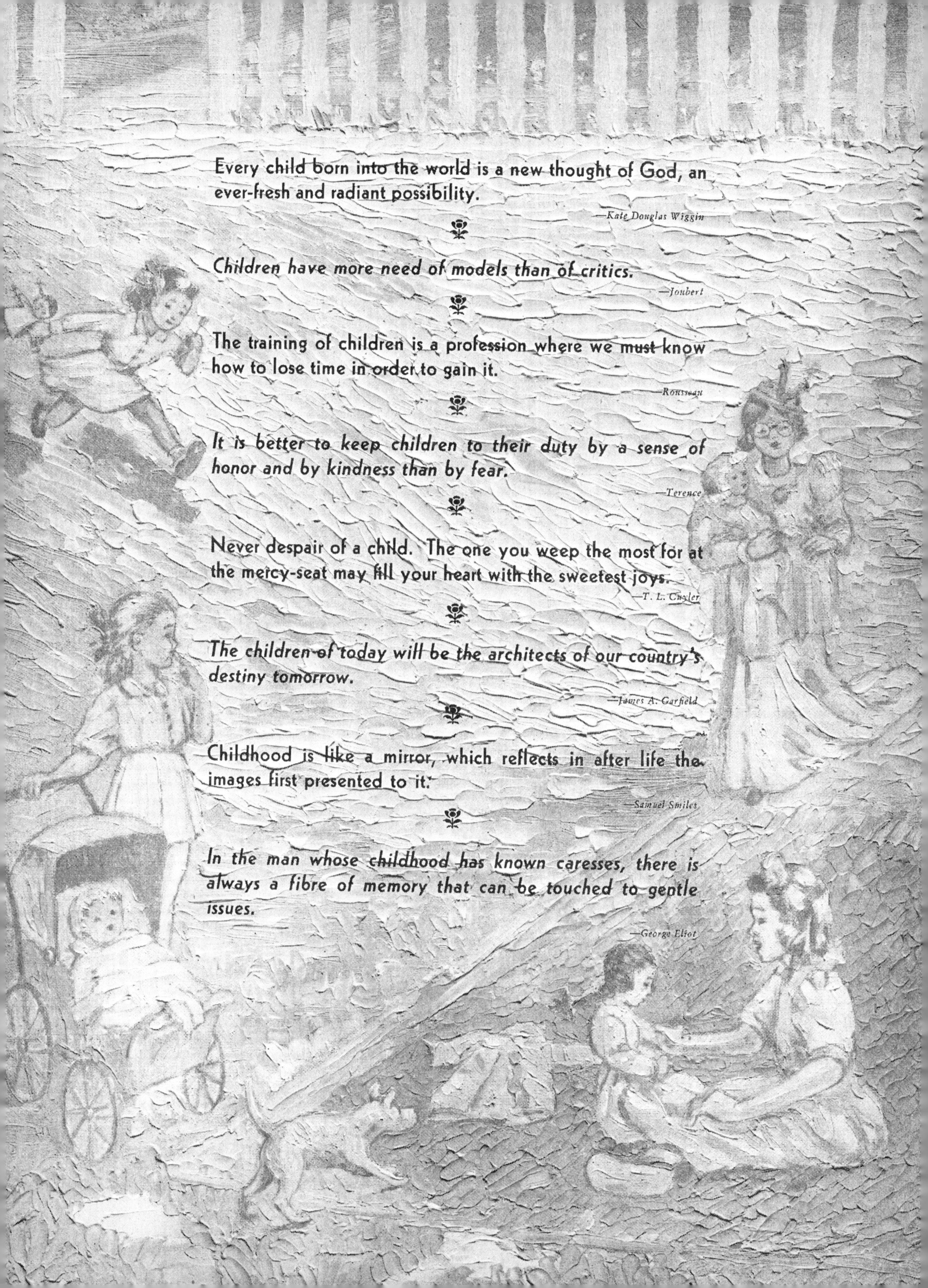

Every child born into the world is a new thought of God, an ever-fresh and radiant possibility.

—Kate Douglas Wiggin

✿

Children have more need of models than of critics.

—Joubert

✿

The training of children is a profession where we must know how to lose time in order to gain it.

—Rousseau

✿

It is better to keep children to their duty by a sense of honor and by kindness than by fear.

—Terence

✿

Never despair of a child. The one you weep the most for at the mercy-seat may fill your heart with the sweetest joys.

—T. L. Cuyler

✿

The children of today will be the architects of our country's destiny tomorrow.

—James A. Garfield

✿

Childhood is like a mirror, which reflects in after life the images first presented to it.

—Samuel Smiles

✿

In the man whose childhood has known caresses, there is always a fibre of memory that can be touched to gentle issues.

—George Eliot

Ideals 1980 Mother's Day Plate Reservation Certificate

Please reserve _____ personal edition(s) of the 1980 Mother's Day Plate, bearing the original work of art by Frances Hook at the original issue price of $29.95, plus $1.50 postage and handling. I have enclosed a total of $31.45* (payment in full) as indicated: 27962

☐ CHECK   ☐ MONEY ORDER   PLEASE CHARGE MY ☐   MASTER CHARGE

BP03   Remit In U.S. Funds   ☐   BANKAMERICARD/VISA

NAME _____   Signature _____

ADDRESS _____   Account No. [ ][ ][ ][ ][ ][ ][ ][ ][ ][ ][ ][ ][ ][ ]

CITY _____

STATE _____ ZIP _____   Expires [ ][ ][ ][ ]

*Wisconsin Residents Add 4% ($1.20) Sales Tax   All Orders Subject To Approval

FOLD HERE FIRST

FOLD SIDE FLAPS FIRST — THEN FOLD HERE

from

( ) _____

ZIP CODE

ideals
PUBLISHING CORPORATION
175 COMMUNITY DRIVE
GREAT NECK, NEW YORK 11025

THANK YOU!

When properly folded with the above gummed flap and its contents will travel safely through the mail.

FOLD HERE FIRST

ABOUT THE PLATE: "MOTHERS OVER THE FENCE"

The painting featured on the 1980 Ideals Mother's Day Plate originally appeared in a 1966 issue of *Ideals* magazine. The editors of Ideals, in concert with the artist, utilized their talents to produce a visual representation of the warmth and friendliness exhibited by mothers and children everywhere.

The painting was originally done in 1965, a period during which this country experienced a great deal of political and social unrest. With that in mind,

models were posed in a setting and dressed in a mode which depicted an earlier and somewhat more tranquil place and time.

The end result was and is an exquisite painting depicting the warmth of neighboring mothers and their children while blending the delights of real life within a framework of delicate fantasy.

Appropriately, this 1980 Mother's Day Plate acknowledges the many mothers who embody warmth, love, and neighborliness.